Accounting and Reporting by Charities
in the
Republic of Ireland

GW00362611

Accounting and Reporting by Charities
in the
Republic of Ireland

Teresa Harrington

Published by
Chartered Accountants Ireland
Chartered Accountants House
47–49 Pearse Street
Dublin 2
www.charteredaccountants.ie

ISBN: 978-1-907214-31-8

Typeset by Amnet
Printed by MPG

CONTENTS

PREFACE

This book provides guidance for those responsible for the preparation of financial statements for charities in the Republic of Ireland. It is written at a time when the charity sector in Ireland awaits the commencement of major sections of the Charities Act 2009. Sections 50 and 51, once commenced, will have a significant impact on the financial reporting requirements of charities.

Preparers of charity accounts and reports should ensure that they keep abreast of changes announced and, in particular, the commencement dates of the individual sections of the Act.

ACKNOWLEDGEMENTS

I would like to express my thanks and appreciation to my colleagues at PwC who facilitated and encouraged me throughout this project, in particular to Declan McKeon and Fiona Hackett for their technical assistance and guidance, and to Aisling Fitzgerald who assisted me in the research for this book.

Chapter 1

INTRODUCTION

The publication of the Charities Act 2009 ('The Act') on 28 February 2009 has focused attention on the form and content of charity accounts and reports. The Charities Act (section 48(1)) provides that the trustees of a charitable organisation shall, in respect of each financial year, prepare a statement of accounts in such form and content as may be prescribed by regulations made by the Minister. Section 52(1) of the Act provides that the trustees of a charity shall prepare and submit an annual report to the Charity Regulator in accordance with regulations made by the Minister. These regulations have not yet been developed and the Minister has undertaken to consult with the Charity Sector in that regard. **1.1**

In tandem with the change in charity law in Ireland, the nature of UK and Irish Generally Accepted Accounting Practice (UK/Irish GAAP) is changing. All EU-listed companies since 2005 have to prepare their consolidated financial statements using International Financial Reporting Standards (IFRS). Unlisted companies, groups, entities and charities who are required to prepare financial statements that give a true and fair view continue to prepare them using Irish GAAP. In 2009, the International Accounting Standards Board (IASB) published the IFRS for SMEs. This is a stand-alone standard that is aimed at private companies. The IFRS for SMEs is less onerous and more user-friendly than full IFRS and is therefore more attractive to private companies. Leveraging off the IASB's IFRS for SMEs, the Accounting Standards Board (ASB) sought comments on its proposals that current UK and Irish GAAP will, for all but very small companies, be replaced by full IFRS or IFRS for SMEs in the near future. **1.2**

There has been considerable debate as to whether the IASB Framework adequately addresses public benefit entity issues. IFRS are not framed with public benefit entities in mind and they were not designed to apply to those entities. National **1.3** standard setters are considering the implications of converging with IFRS for these entities. In August 2009, the ASB issued a consultation paper, *Policy Proposal: The Future of UK GAAP,* and requested comments on the policy proposal. As part of this consultation process the ASB sought views on whether converged UK/Irish GAAP should be supplemented if it is to provide an adequate and practicable accounting framework for public benefit entities and reduce the risk of inconsistent accounting practices arising within the sector and undue complexity in reporting. The ASB has set out a number of options for dealing with public benefit entities that are required to prepare financial statements intended to give a true and fair view under converged UK and Irish GAAP. In the consultation paper a public benefit entity is defined as:

> "an entity that is organised and operated primarily for community or social benefit whose funders and other resource providers do not receive any financial return from the organisation and any surpluses are applied to support the objectives of the entity".

(Source: *Policy Proposal: The Future of UK GAAP,* page 33, paragraph 3.5)

Charities fall within this definition.

1.4 The ASB identified four main options for dealing with public benefit issues under converged UK GAAP as set out in paragraph 3.12 of the consultation paper as follows:

> "i. A public benefit entity framework, similar to the Interpretation – covering principles but not specific accounting requirements;
>
> ii. A public benefit (not-for-profit) standard – setting out where different accounting is required for public benefit entities;
>
> iii. Separate standards on public benefit issues – for example a standard on contributions, a standard on fund accounting, a standard on the presentation of the primary statements, etc.;
>
> iv. Supplementary text in UK GAAP – for example separate paragraphs, or Application Notes, in a fixed asset

standard on measuring the service potential of assets, or in a business combinations standard on acquisitions at nil or nominal value or merger accounting."

The ASB is working through the responses received.

Currently, in England and Wales, the best practice recommenda-   **1.5**
tions adopted by charities for the form and content of their financial statements, trustees' report and accompanying information,
are contained in the *Statement of Recommended Practice: Accounting
and Reporting by Charities* (SORP) which is underpinned by law.
Trustees of charities that are companies should include any
additional information that is required by law in order for their
financial statements to comply with statutory requirements.

The Charity Commission for England and Wales published the
SORP, *Accounting by Charities*, in October 1995. A revised version
was published in October 2000 and called *Statement of
Recommended Practice – Accounting and Reporting by Charities*.
This SORP was revised and published during 2005 (thus referred
to here as 'SORP 2005'). The objectives of the SORP as set out in
the Introduction to the SORP 2005 (paragraph 2) are as
follows:

"(a) improving the quality of financial reporting by
      charities;
 (b) enhancing the relevance, comparability and under-
      standability of information presented in accounts;
 (c) providing clarification, explanation and interpretation
      of accounting standards and of their application in the
      charities sector and to sector specific transactions; and
      thereby;
 (d) assisting those who are responsible for the preparation
      of the Trustees' Annual Report and Accounts."

Irish charities, in the absence of regulations governing the financial reporting requirements of charities, may consider the
requirements of the SORP as representing best practice. SORP
2005 has been adopted by a number of charities in the Republic
of Ireland and this book deals with a number of practical aspects
of adoption of the financial accounting requirements of the
SORP in Ireland. Irish charities that are companies should

comply with their statutory obligations under the Companies Acts 1963 to 2009.

1.6   The purpose of this publication is to set out an analysis and discussion of Generally Accepted Accounting Practice in Ireland ('Irish GAAP') as it applies to charities in the Republic of Ireland. In the Republic of Ireland there is currently no specific format for the accounts and reports of charities. In the UK the format of accounts for all charities is guided by the *Statement of Recommended Practice (SORP 2005): Accounting and Reporting by Charities* (Revised 2005) and by Acts governing charities in England and Wales, Scotland and Northern Ireland.

Chapter 2

CHARITIES ACT 2009

INTRODUCTION

The Charities Act 2009 ('The Act') was signed into law by **2.1** President Mary McAleese on 28 February 2009. The Act will only come into force when the Minister introduces commencement orders for the individual provisions and sections. The Act includes (for the first time in primary legislation) a definition of "charitable purpose" which is set out at section 3 as:

(a) the prevention or relief of poverty or economic hardship;
(b) the advancement of education;
(c) the advancement of religion;
(d) any other purpose that is of benefit to the community.

The Act states that a purpose will not be a charitable purpose **2.2** unless it is of *public benefit*.

The Act provides for the establishment of the Charities Regulatory **2.3** Authority (CRA) and the appointment of a regulator. The CRA will establish and maintain a register of charitable organisations. The Act imposes annual reporting requirements on charities and a brief summary of these requirements is outlined in this chapter.

When the Act comes into force, charities will be required to: **2.4**

- register with the Charity Regulator;
- provide annual reports and annual financial returns to the CRA;
- obtain permits for all types of fundraising;
- provide details of fundraising activities in the annual report;
- follow agreed codes of practice for fundraising from the public.

2.5 Trustee duties, responsibilities and liabilities are set out in the Act and the Act permits the purchase of trustee indemnity insurance by the charity.

2.6 A timetable for the introduction of Commencement Orders has not yet been published. At the time of writing six sections of the Act have been commenced, namely:

Section 2 of the Act which contains the definitions of certain terms used in the Act.
Section 4 – Orders and Regulations, which allows the Minister to make Regulations under The Act.
Section 5, a technical section which provides that expenses incurred by the Minister in the administration of the Act shall be paid out of moneys provided by the Oireachtas.
Section 10, which sets out the possible penalties on conviction for a breach of section 99.
Section 90, which will grant power to the courts, in the event of proceedings against a charity trustee, to grant relief to such trustees from personal liability for breach of trust, where it appears to the relevant court that the trustee acted honestly and reasonably.
Section 99 – Mass cards, which makes it an offence for a Mass card to be sold in contravention of the provisions of section 99 of the Act.

REGISTRATION

2.7 The register of charities will be established and maintained by the CRA. A charitable organisation must apply for registration with the regulator within six months after the commencement of the relevant section of the Act. If the charity has already been granted charitable tax status by the Revenue Commissioners that charity will be automatically registered with the CRA. The Revenue Commissioners will continue to deal with and grant tax exempt status to qualifying charities, and the determination of charitable status for the purpose of the Charity Act will rest with the CRA. Situations could arise whereby an organisation may be granted charitable status by the CRA but not be granted charitable tax status by the Revenue Commissioners.

ACCOUNTING AND REPORTING

Sections 47 to 54 of the Act set out the requirements on charities **2.8** in respect of accounting and reporting. Section 47 sets out the requirements for the keeping of proper books of account and requires that the books of account must be maintained in sufficient detail that they will enable the trustees to prepare financial statements that will give a true and fair view of the state of affairs of the charity and explain its transactions.

Section 48 sets out the requirement to prepare an annual state- **2.9** ment of accounts (financial statements) in accordance with the Regulations to be made by the Minister. Where gross income or expenditure is €100,000 or less, the charity may prepare an income expenditure account and a statement of assets and liabilities. The form of these accounts (financial statements) will also be prescribed by the Minister.

AUDIT AND INDEPENDENT EXAMINATION

Section 50 of the Act sets out the requirements for audit or inde- **2.10** pendent examination of the financial statements of charity organisations. Where the gross income or expenditure of the charity exceeds a threshold to be determined by the Minister (but not to exceed €500,000) the charity will be required to have its financial statements audited; where the gross income or expenditure is below this amount an independent examination will be required. Charities with a gross income or expenditure of less than €10,000 (or up to a maximum of €50,000) will not be required to submit audited or examined financial statements to the regulator. Section 50 does not apply to educational bodies.

In the case of charities that are incorporated under the Companies **2.11** Acts 1963 to 2009 the provisions of those Acts will continue to apply. Section 49 of the Act makes provision for the Registrar of Companies to make the Annual Return and related documents available to the CRA.

Section 51 of the Act sets out the powers of the Minister and the **2.12** CRA to make regulations in relation to audit and independent examination.

ANNUAL RETURNS AND ANNUAL ACTIVITY REPORTS

2.13 Within 10 months of the financial year end, a charity must submit a report of its activities in that year to the CRA – the report is referred to as the 'Annual Report'. The form of this report will be prescribed by the Minister by regulation. The information required may vary, depending on the different classes of information and different classes of organisation.

2.14 The following information should be attached to the Annual Return:

- a copy of the annual financial statements or income and expenditure and statement of assets and liabilities;
- a copy of the auditors' report where the financial statements are required to be audited;
- a copy of the independent examiner's report where the accounts have been examined rather than audited;
- financial statements prepared in accordance with the Companies Acts where the charity is an incorporated charity. (This applies even where the charity company is not required to file its financial statements with the Companies Registration Office (CRO).)

2.15 The Act provides that there will be public access to the information on the CRA website with certain limited exceptions. Charities that are private charitable trusts do not have to comply with this requirement (see section 54(2), Charities Act 2009). A private charitable trust is one that is not funded by way of donations from the public. The exemption relates only to publication of the private charity's annual report and documents attached to the Annual Report filed with the Charity Register.

Chapter 3

SORP – ACCOUNTING AND REPORTING BY CHARITIES

INTRODUCTION

The format of the accounts of charities in the UK is guided by the **3.1** *Statement of Recommended Practice – Accounting and Reporting by Charities* (Revised 2005) (SORP) issued by the UK Charity Commission in conjunction with the ASB. The accounting recommendations of SORP 2005 apply to all charities in the UK that prepare financial statements under the accruals basis of accounting to give a true and fair view of the charity's activities and financial position regardless of their size, constitution and complexity. In England and Wales, the recommendations for the form and content of the financial statements, trustees' report and accompanying information is underpinned by law. The UK Charity Commission provide examples of Trustees' Annual Reports and Accounts at www.charity-commission.gov.uk (charity accounting and reporting). These provide useful guidance for Irish charities. However, not all disclosures required under UK charity law are provided for in the Irish Charities Act 2009.

In Ireland, the Charities Act 2009 (section 48(1)) provides that the form and content of charity financial statements should conform to those that may be prescribed by regulations made by the Minister. These sections of the Charities Act 2009 have not yet commenced and the regulations have not been developed by the Minister.

The SORP moves away from the concept of profit and maximis- **3.2** ing shareholder value as a measure of success or failure of a charity. Instead, it focuses on the overall objective of charities to use their resources in furtherance of their charitable objects and maximising the impact of their actions and use of resources for the benefit of their beneficiaries. For this reason, the SORP requires that all income of the charity should be recognised as incoming resources of the charity in the **Statement of Financial Activities ('SOFA')**.

STATUS OF THE SORP IN THE REPUBLIC OF IRELAND

3.3   Charities in the Republic of Ireland do not fall within the scope of the SORP. They may, however, choose to comply with its recommendations. If charities in the Republic of Ireland choose to adopt the SORP's recommendations, they are encouraged to disclose that fact in their financial statements.

CHARITABLE COMPANIES IN THE REPUBLIC OF IRELAND

3.4   Charities in the Republic of Ireland that are also limited companies, and who are considering applying the SORP, will need to have regard to their own circumstances when considering the application of the Companies Acts 1963 to 2009. In following the SORP, charitable companies will generally meet most of the requirements under the Companies Acts; however, certain requirements, including the requirement to produce a profit and loss account will also require to be addressed if applying the SORP.

3.5   Incorporated charities are required to prepare financial statements that give a true and fair view of the result for the year and of the state of affairs of the company at the balance sheet date. These companies must have regard to a number of items that would not normally be included in a profit and loss account prepared in accordance with the Companies Acts, but which are included in a Statement of Financial Activities ('SOFA') under the SORP, including:

- unrealised gains and losses arising during the year;
- capital grants; and
- movement on endowment (capital) funds during the year.

3.6   The SOFA is designed to include all of the gains and losses of a charity that would be included in the profit and loss account and the Statement of Total Recognised Gains and Losses (STRGL) as required by FRS 3. Unrealised gains and losses on investments are not recognised in the profit and loss account under the Companies Acts. However, they are included in the SOFA. Capital grants are accounted for in accordance with Statement of Standard Accounting Practice 4 – Accounting for

Government Grants under the Companies Acts, and are treated as deferred credits in the balance sheet and credited to the profit and loss account over the estimated useful life of the related asset.

If the charity is not in receipt of capital grants and does not hold endowment funds or investments, the company may not need to produce a separate profit and loss account, but the headings used in the SOFA should be changed so that the title clearly indicates that it includes a profit and loss account and a STRGL (if required), and there is a prominent sub-total entitled: "Net Profit/(Loss) for the Year" which either replaces or is in addition to the heading of "Net Incoming Resources".   **3.7**

TRUSTEES' ANNUAL REPORT

The SORP requires the trustees of charities to prepare a Trustees' Annual Report and encourages a structured and focused approach to reporting. The purpose of the Trustees' Annual Report is to provide the trustees with an opportunity to explain areas of the activities and objectives of the charity that the financial statements alone cannot convey. Good reporting by a charity will explain 'what the charity is trying to do and how it is going about it'. The governance and management structure of the charity should also be explained in the Trustees' Annual Report.   **3.8**

Responsibility for preparing the report rests with the trustees of the charity. Additional information, such as a chairman's report and reports from individual departments or functions within the charity's structure, may also be incorporated into the annual report. The information disclosed must be consistent with that shown in the financial statements.   **3.9**

The SORP recommends seven headings to provide the information required in the Trustees' Annual Report as follows: **3.10**

- Reference and Administrative Details of the Charity, its Trustees and Advisers
- Structure, Governance and Management
- Objectives and Activities

- Achievements and Performance
- Financial Review
- Plans for Future Periods
- Funds Held as Custodian Trustee on Behalf of Others

The detail included under each heading will vary, depending on the size of the charity and the complexity of its activities. Examples of the type of information to be included under each heading are set out below:

Reference and Administrative Details of the Charity, its Trustees and Advisers

- The address of the principal office of the charity, and the registered office of the charity if it is a company.
- The names of all the trustees on the date of approval of the report and those who served during the financial year.
- The name of any chief executive officer or other senior staff members to whom day-to-day management of the charity is delegated by the charity trustees.
- The names and addresses of any other relevant organisations or persons, including bankers, solicitors, auditors (or independent examiner or reporting accountant) and investment or other principal advisers.

Structure, Governance and Management

- The nature of the governing document and how the charity is constituted.
- The methods used to recruit and appoint new trustees, including any constitutional provisions.
- The name of any person or body external to the charity entitled to appoint one or more of the trustees where applicable.
- The policies and procedures adopted for the induction and training of trustees.
- The relationship of the charity with any wider network (e.g. charities affiliated within an umbrella group) and any impact of this network on the operating policies of the charity.
- The relationship between the charity and related parties including its subsidiaries and with any other charities and

organisations with which it cooperates in the pursuit of its charitable objectives.
- A statement that the major risks to which the charity is exposed, as identified by the trustees, have been reviewed and systems or procedures have been established to manage those risks.

Objectives and Activities

- A summary of the objects of the charity as set out in the governing document.
- An explanation of the charity's aims including the changes or differences it seeks to make through its activities.
- An explanation of the charity's strategies for achieving its stated objectives.
- Details of the significant activities that contribute to the achievement of the stated objectives.
- Activities undertaken to further a charity's purposes for the benefit of the public.
- Where the charity conducts a material part of its activities through grant making, a statement setting out its grant-making policies.
- Where significant use is made of volunteers to undertake charitable or income-generating activities, an explanation of their role and contribution.

Achievements and Performance

- A review of charitable activities undertaken that explains the performance achieved against objectives set, including a summary of the qualitative and quantitative measures or indicators used to assess these achievements, where applicable.
- Where material fundraising activities are undertaken, details of the performance achieved against fundraising objectives set, including commentary on any material expenditure for future income generation and explaining the effect on current period's fundraising return and the anticipated future income generation.
- Where material investments are held, details of the investment performance achieved against the investment objectives set.

- Commentary on those factors, within and outside the charity's control, which are relevant to the achievement of its objectives, e.g. relationships with employees, users, beneficiaries, funders and the charity's position in the wider community.

Financial Review

- The Trustees' Annual Report should contain a review of the financial position of the charity and a statement of the charity's policies, in particular:
  - The charity's policy on reserves stating the level of reserves held and why they are held, including any material funds that are designated. The policy should quantify and explain the purpose of the designated funds, where they are set aside for future expenditure, and the likely timing of that expenditure should also be explained.
  - Principal funding sources and how expenditure in the year under review has supported the key objectives of the charity.

Plans for Future Periods

- Explain the charity's plans for the future, including the aims and key objectives set for future periods and details of any activities planned to achieve them.

Funds Held as Custodian Trustee on Behalf of Others

- Where the charity is, or trustees are, acting as custodian trustees, a description of the assets which they hold in this capacity, the name and objects of the charity on whose behalf the assets are held and how this activity falls within their own objects. The arrangements for safe custody and segregation of such assets from the charity's own assets should also be disclosed.

(**Note:** funds held as custodian should **not** be included in the balance sheet but disclosed in a note to the financial statements.)

Chapter 4

STATEMENT OF FINANCIAL ACTIVITIES (SOFA)

INTRODUCTION

The basic objective of the Statement of Financial Activities (SOFA) is to bring together all of the funds available to the charity and demonstrate how these have been used to meet the charity's objectives. The SOFA should clearly show all of the activities undertaken by the charity and the terms used to describe the activities should mirror those used to describe the incoming resources as far as possible. **4.1**

The SOFA is structured to show whether there has been a net inflow or outflow of funds and provides a reconciliation of all movements in the charity's funds. The form of the SOFA is set out at Table 3 of the SORP, which is reproduced overleaf. The SOFA should be supported by appropriate notes to the financial statements as may be required in order that the financial statements give a true and fair view and enable the user of the charity accounts to gain a proper understanding of the activities and resources of the charity. **4.2**

SORP 2005: Table 3 – Statement of Financial Activities

		Unre-stricted Funds €	Restricted Funds €	Endow-ment Funds €	Total Funds €	Prior Year Total Funds €	SORP Refer-ence
A	**Incoming resources**						
A1	Incoming resources from generated funds						
A1a	Voluntary income						121–136
A1b	Activities for generating funds						137–139
A1c	Investment income						140–142
A2	Incoming resources from charitable activities						143–146
A3	Other incoming resources						147
	Total incoming resources						
B	**Resources expended**						178–179
B1	Costs of generating funds						
B1a	Costs of generating voluntary income						180–184
B1b	Fundraising trading: cost of goods sold and other costs						185–186
B1c	Investment management costs						187
B2	Charitable activities						188–209
B3	Governance costs						210–212
B4	Other resources expended						213
	Total resources expended						
	Net incoming/outgoing resources before transfers						

SORP 2005: Table 3 – *cont.*

Transfers

C	Gross transfers between funds					214–216
	Net incoming resources before other recognised gains and losses					

D	Other recognised gains/ losses					
D1	Gains on revaluation of fixed assets for charity's own use					217–218
D2	Gains/losses on investment assets					219
D3	Actuarial gains/losses on defined benefit pension schemes					220
	Net movement in funds					

E	Reconciliation of Funds				
	Total funds brought forward				
	Total funds carried forward				

Note: References in this chapter to the different SOFA categories will include, where appropriate, the reference numbers shown in the table above.

INCOMING RESOURCES

General Principles for Recognition of Income

The general principles for recognition of income in the financial   **4.3**
statements mean that, where sufficient evidence exists that the
effect of a transaction is to increase the charity's assets, the
income should be recognised. The following three conditions
should be met before income is recognised:

Entitlement: The charity should be entitled to the income.
Entitlement normally arises when the charity
has control over the income and its future use.

Certainty: It should be virtually certain that the income will be received. If the uncertainty relating to the receipt of income cannot be reduced to an acceptable level, income recognition should be deferred until such time as the uncertainty has been reduced to an acceptable level.

Measurement: Income should be recognised when it can be measured with sufficient reliability. Charities will need to select a measurement basis and attribute a monetary amount to income.

Conditional Versus Restricted

4.4 It is important to draw a distinction between restrictions on income and conditions attaching to income. Restrictions on income limit the use of the donated income or asset and the type of expenditure that can be incurred. Restricted income should be recognised when the charity is entitled to the income with reasonable certainty, there has been a transfer of economic benefit and it is measureable.

4.5 In determining whether to recognise income, regard must be had to any conditions attaching to that income. Conditions attaching to income create a barrier that must be overcome before the income can be used and such income should not be recognised until the condition has been met. The transfer of economic benefit to the charity is only met on fulfilment of the condition and the income becoming unconditional.

4.6 The overriding principle is that income should not be recognised until the conditions for its receipt have been met. For example, if the payment of the second instalment of a grant is dependent on the outcome of a review of an activity report on the use of the first instalment, a condition may exist that would prevent recognition of the full grant.

INCOMING RESOURCES (A)

4.7 The recommendations relating to incoming resources are set out at paragraphs 94 to 147 of SORP 2005. 'Incoming resources' has a broader definition than 'income', as it includes 'gifts in kind', 'intangible income' and 'new endowments'. The incoming resources of a charity should be analysed according to the activity that has given rise to the resources. In most cases, it will be clear which activity has generated the resources. The SOFA is structured to show three headings for incoming resources as follows:

- Incoming Resources from Generated Funds (A1)
- Incoming Resources from Charitable Activities (A2)
- Other Incoming Resources (A3)

Incoming resources from *generated funds* are funds raised from activities undertaken by the charity to generate funds that will be used to carry out its charitable activities. Incoming resources from *charitable activities*, on the other hand, are funds generated as a payment for goods and services provided to the charity's beneficiaries. *Other incoming resources* are all other sources of income that do not readily fall within the previous two headings.

In situations where income is generated from a number of different activities, the SORP provides that it is permissible to apportion the resources between the activities on a 'reasonable, justifiable and consistent' basis.   4.8

INCOMING RESOURCES FROM GENERATED FUNDS (A1)

The most common types of incoming resources from generated funds by charities are: 4.9

- Voluntary Income (A1a)
- Activities for Generating Funds (A1b)
- Investment Income (A1c)

Voluntary Income – (A1a)

Voluntary income is defined in the Glossary to the SORP (Appendix 1) at GL 61 as follows: 4.10

"Voluntary income comprises gifts that will not normally provide any return to the donor other than the knowledge that someone will benefit from the donation.

This will exclude any gifts that are quasi-contractual (in that a certain service to a certain level must be provided) but they would include gifts that must be spent on some particular area of work (i.e. restricted funds) or given to be held as endowment. Voluntary income will normally include gifts in kind and donated services, for example gifts in kind as part of an international programme."

Voluntary income includes incoming resources from the following:

- donations (see **paragraph 4.12**);
- gifts-in-kind (see **paragraphs 4.13–4.21**);
- legacy income (see **paragraphs 4.22–4.24**);
- grant income (see **paragraphs 4.25–4.29**);
- membership subscriptions (see **paragraph 4.30**).

4.11 Details of activities undertaken to generate voluntary income should be provided either on the face of the SOFA or in the notes to the financial statements. The analysis categories should, as far as possible, match the detailed analysis provided for the costs of generating voluntary income. The accounting policies adopted for each significant source of income should be set out in the statement of accounting policies.

Donations

4.12 Donations are generally either cash donations or donations-in-kind. The accounting for cash donations is straightforward; they should be recognised when the charity becomes entitled to them and there is reasonable certainty that they will be received. This income source would include amounts received under committed giving.

Also included in this category of incoming resources is income raised from street collections and other cash collections/appeals. It is incumbent on the trustees of charities to ensure that proper controls are in place over the collection, recording and application of monies raised. The CRA will require information from charities concerning their fundraising activities in their applications for registration as well as in their annual return and financial statements.

Non-statutory codes of good practice for fundraising have been developed by ICTR (Irish Charities Tax Research) in partnership with the Department of Community, Equality and Gaeltacht Affairs. Section 97 of the Charities Act 2009 provides that the Minister may regulate fundraising if he is dissatisfied with the manner in which charities fundraise.

Gifts-in-kind

Many charities receive gifts (donations) in kind, being the receipt of assets as donations rather than cash. These can take many forms: **4.13**

- buildings or equipment (see **paragraphs 4.15–4.16**);
- donated services or facilities (see **paragraphs 4.17–4.19**);
- goods for distribution (see **paragraphs 4.20–4.21**).

Because these transactions have an economic impact on the charity, they should be reflected in the financial statements. In practice, however, it may not be possible to measure some services with sufficient reliability and in that case they should not be recognised. The notes to the financial statements could provide details of these services where the information is considered useful to the users of the financial statements.   **4.14**

Buildings or Equipment Where assets such as buildings, equipment or motor vehicles are donated to a charity, these should be included in the SOFA as incoming resources and as additions to fixed assets in the balance sheet. They should be included at their current value at the date of the gift or donation. These should be depreciated in the same way as assets acquired by the charity.   **4.15**

Where a charity is an incorporated entity, it may need to produce a separate profit and loss account that would exclude the unrealised gain on the donation, because such unrealised gains are not included in the profit and loss account under the Companies Acts, which provide that only realised profits at the balance sheet date should be included in the profit and loss account. The asset should be recognised at nil cost, revalued at the date of the gift or donation and the revaluation surplus should be included in the STRGL. The related depreciation should be charged to the profit and loss account.

4.16   In each case, the donated assets should be valued at a reasonable estimate of their value to the charity. This value can be determined by reference to the donor or to an external source of information.

4.17   *Donated services and facilities* Some charities receive certain services on a pro-bono basis (e.g. accounting services or legal and other professional advice). These services, which would normally have been purchased, should be valued based on the estimated value to the charity. This could be determined by estimating the amount saved by not paying for the service by reference to the supplier of the service or by past experience. A corresponding amount should be included in expenditure.

4.18   Where an individual provides a service that would normally be purchased by a charity, this should be measured and recognised. Where a group of individuals/volunteers provide a service (e.g. visiting and assisting clients at a hospice or care facility), this may not be a service that the charity would normally provide and there may be difficulties in measuring the value of the service in monetary terms with sufficient reliability; therefore, these would not be recognised. The charity SORP excludes the valuation of 'general' volunteer services.

4.19   A charity may also receive assistance in the form of donated facilities, e.g. free occupation of a building. The amount to be recognised as income and a corresponding expense should be the estimated value to the charity of the facility received, e.g. market rent for space occupied.

4.20   *Goods for distribution* Charities that receive goods for distribution, for example, overseas development charities who receive donated goods that they can then distribute to people who are the beneficiaries of the charity, should recognise these as income where the value of goods is material. They should be valued at either their value to the charity as a result of costs saved or at a third-party value if such can be obtained. A corresponding amount should be included in expenditure. The income and the expense should be recognised in the year in which the goods are distributed.

An example of the accounting policy for donated goods taken from the UK Charity Commission website is set out below:

"Donated goods are recognised in different ways dependent on how they are used by the charity:

(i) Those donated for resale produce income in the trading subsidiary are recognised when they are disposed of.
(ii) Those donated for onward transmission to beneficiaries (chiefly clothing, food and medical supplies) are included in the statement of financial activities as incoming resources and resources expended when they are distributed. They are valued at the amount the charity would have had to pay to acquire them at the time of donation."

(Source: UK Charity Commission website (www.charity-commission.gov.uk): Commentary on the Model Trustees' Annual Report and Accounts: Aid Overseas)

In all cases, the basis of valuation and accounting for gifts-in-kind should be disclosed in the financial statements. Where material, an adjustment should be made to the original valuation upon subsequent realisation of the gift.   **4.21**

Where there are undistributed goods/assets at the year end, a description of the items, a reasonable estimate of the value of the goods/assets, should be included in the notes to the financial statements.

Where the nature and scale of volunteer services is significant and would help the reader of the financial statements, information on these services should also be disclosed either in the notes or in other information accompanying the financial statements. Many charities disclose immaterial donations and gifts as an acknowledgement of the gift or donation.

Legacy income

Legacy income should be recognised on a receivable basis where there is virtual certainty that the legacy will be received and the value of the legacy can be measured with sufficient reliability. These criteria will normally be met following probate and once the executors have established that there are sufficient assets in the estate, after liabilities, to pay the legacy.   **4.22**

Where a notice of a legacy is received after the charity's year end, but it is clear that the executors have agreed prior to year end that the legacy can be paid, the income should be accrued. The measurement of the amount receivable should take account of valuations and possible disputes.

4.23 There will normally be sufficient certainty of receipt when notice of intention to pay out the legacy is received from the personal representative of the estate. It is likely that the value of the receipt can also be reliably measured at that time. However, in situations where the legacy is not immediately payable, such legacies should not be recognised until the conditions for receipt have been satisfied, e.g. the death of a life tenant.

4.24 Where the charity has been notified of a material legacy and the conditions attaching to that legacy have not been met at the balance sheet date, the notes to the financial statements should disclose this fact and provide a reasonable estimate of the amount where possible. The accounting policy in respect of donations should also be disclosed.

Grant income

4.25 Grant income received is analysed in the SOFA as either voluntary income or incoming resources from charitable activities, depending upon the character of the grant. Grants that do not create a service requirement should be recognised as voluntary income. The general rules for recognition of income – entitlement, certainty and measurement – apply equally to grant income recognition. The key element to consider is whether the charity has entitlement to the income. Entitlement will normally exist when the grant is formally approved in writing and conditions attaching to the grant have been met or there is virtual certainty that they will be met.

4.26 Where there are no conditions attaching to the grant, and the charity has discretion over the timing of expenditure, it should be recognised immediately in its entirety, once the criteria of certainty and measurability are met. This may result in situations where the grant income is recognised in an earlier period than the expenditure to which it relates. However, these grants should not be deferred simply because the expenditure has not been incurred.

This treatment differs from the accounting treatment adopted by companies. Under the Statement of Standard Accounting Practice (SSAP) 4, the accounting standard that deals with grants, grant income is recognised in the same period as the related expenditure. Capital grants, accounted for under SSAP 4, should be treated as deferred credits of which a proportion would be credited to income annually as the related asset is depreciated. Under the requirements of the SORP, capital grants are recognised as incoming resources in the period in which the charity becomes entitled to the grant and the other conditions for income recognition are met.

In the UK, the SORP is underpinned by law. Charities that are companies must comply with the SORP and therefore follow the accounting treatment prescribed by it. In Ireland, charities that are companies and those whose financial statements are required to give a true and fair view must comply with SSAP 4. These charities who wish to comply with the SORP in Ireland may need to consider whether to do so impacts on the true and fair view given by the financial statements and may need to avail of the true and fair view override provisions of the Companies Acts (see **Chapter 9, paragraph 9.4** below).

Charities often receive grants with conditions attached that must **4.27** be fulfilled before the charity has unconditional entitlement to the grant. In these cases, where meeting the conditions is within the charity's control and there is sufficient evidence that these conditions will be met, then the grant should be recognised.

In cases where meeting the conditions is not within the charity's control, e.g. raising matching funds, the grant should not be recognised until the condition has been met and it should be deferred as a liability until such time as the conditions have been met.

Grants may also be subject to conditions that specify the time period during which the grant may be spent and in such cases the charity's ability to spend the grant is restricted and the grant should not be recognised until such time as the charity is allowed to spend it. Where the existence of a condition prevents the recognition of grant income, a contingent asset should be disclosed in the notes to the financial statements where it is probable (but not virtually certain) that the conditions will be met in the future.

4.28 Voluntary income includes grants that are provided by government or a charitable foundation for core funding, or are of a general nature, but does not include grants that are specifically for the performance of a service or production of charitable goods. Restricted grants that do not create a service requirement are normally analysed as restricted voluntary income.

4.29 Where any grants (or incoming resources) are deferred, the notes to the financial statements should explain the reasons for the deferral and provide an analysis of the movements from the beginning to the end of the year.

Membership subscriptions

4.30 Some charities may receive membership subscriptions. Where these are in substance a gift to the charity, they should be treated as voluntary income. Where these are connected with the provision of a service, they should be recognised as income from activities to generate funds as the service is delivered. It may be appropriate to recognise the incoming resource on a pro rata basis over the term of the membership where the services are delivered evenly over the term of membership.

Activities for Generating Funds – (A1b)

4.31 *Activities for generating funds* are the trading activities of the charity, such as fundraising, sponsorships and lotteries, which do not fall within the definition of donations. The funds generated will be used to undertake the charitable activities of the charity. The categories of income to be included within this heading in the SOFA are set out at paragraph 137 of the SORP. The included activities involve an element of exchange, with the charity receiving income in return for providing a service, goods, tickets for raffles or events, etc. This category includes:

- fundraising events, sponsorships and social lotteries (see **paragraph 4.32**);
- goods for resale by charity shops (see **paragraph 4.33**);
- providing goods and services other than for the benefit of the charity's beneficiaries (see **paragraph 4.34**);
- letting and licensing arrangements of property (see **paragraph 4.35**).

Fundraising events, sponsorships and social lotteries

Fundraising events such as jumble sales, firework displays and   **4.32**
concerts (which are legally considered to be trading activities)
and sponsorships and social lotteries which cannot be considered as pure donations should be included in the SOFA under
the heading Activities for Generating Funds. They should be
reported on gross when raised by the charity or its agents. Items
received as donations for raffle prizes, auctions, etc. should also
be included in this category.

Goods for resale by charity shops

Goods for resale by charity shops are generally regarded as gifts-in-   **4.33**
kind for subsequent conversion into cash by the charity. These
should be accounted for when the goods are sold and the charity
should recognise the cash as income. The sale of donated goods is
considered to be the realisation of a donation-in-kind in economic
terms and should be included with *Activities for Generating Funds*.

The sale of goods that have been donated to a charity is not trading and differs from the sale of goods and services as part of the
direct charitable activities of the charity (discussed at **paragraph
4.38** below). This is so, even if the goods are sorted, cleaned and
repaired prior to sale. However, if goods are subjected to significant change that brings them to a different condition for sale
than when they were donated they may be regarded as part of
direct charitable activities.

Providing goods and services other than for the benefit of the charity's beneficiaries

Where the charity uses its resources to generate income by pro-   **4.34**
viding goods or services to people other than the charity's
beneficiaries, e.g. workshops, seminars for the public at large
and publishing material in return for a fee, these should be
accounted for as Activities for Generating Funds and recognised
in the SOFA when the charity becomes entitled to the income.

Letting and licensing arrangements of property

Where property held primarily for functional use by the charity,   **4.35**
but temporarily surplus to operational requirements, is let under
a lease or licence arrangement, the income under that arrangement

should be accounted for as income from activities for generating funds when the charity becomes entitled to that income. (For example, if a floor space in a building used by a charity becomes available due to reduced staff numbers and is let to a third party.)

Investment Income – (A1c)

4.36   *Investment income* includes dividends, interest and rents received and receivable. They should be recognised on an accruals basis. Investment income does not include realised and unrealised gains and losses on investments.

If a charity is adopting the Charity SORP and is not an incorporated charity then any gains and losses on investments (including property investments) should be included under the gains and losses on the revaluation and disposal of investment assets section of the SOFA (D2).

If the charity is an Irish incorporated charity, unrealised gains and losses from investments should be recognised in the Statement of Total Recognised Gains and Losses (STRGL).

INCOMING RESOURCES FROM CHARITABLE ACTIVITIES (A2)

4.37   *Incoming resources from charitable activities*, which are discussed at paragraph 143 to 146 of SORP 2005, should include the following:

- the sale of goods and services as part of the direct charitable activities of the charity (known as 'primary purpose trading') and the letting of non-investment property in furtherance of the charity's objectives (see **paragraph 4.38**);
- contractual payments from Government or public authorities, where these are received in the normal course of trading, e.g. fees for respite care (see **paragraph 4.39–4.40**);
- Grants specifically for the provision of goods and services to be provided as part of the charitable activities or services to beneficiaries (see **paragraph 4.41**);
- Ancillary trades connected to a primary purpose (see **paragraph 4.42**).

The sale of goods and services as part of the direct charitable activities of the charity

As an activity, the sale of goods and services as part of the direct charitable activities of the charity is generally known as 'primary purpose trading'. This is trading that contributes directly to one or more of the objects of a charity as set out in the governing document (i.e. its rules or constitution). It includes trading in which the work in connection with the trading is mainly carried out by beneficiaries of the charity. It would include, for example: **4.38**

- sale of goods produced by disabled people who are beneficiaries of a charity for the disabled;
- holding of an exhibition at a charitable art gallery or museum in return for an admission fee;
- provision of residential accommodation by a residential care charity in return for payment;
- provision of educational services by a charitable school or college in return for course fees.

Contractual payments from Government or public authorities where these are received in the normal course of trading

Where a charity enters into a contractual agreement with the Government or an agent of the Government, the income should be recognised when the charity has delivered the goods or services that it has agreed to provide under the terms of the contract.   **4.39**

The SORP recognises that some grants contain conditions that require the performance of a specified service where payment is conditional on a specified output being achieved. These are performance-related grants and have conditions that make them similar in economic terms to economic trading. These are analysed as incoming resources from charitable activities within the SOFA. In the case of performance-related grants, these should be recognised when the charity has performed the services and earned entitlement to the grant, i.e. the income is either accrued or deferred in line with performance.

The terms of the grant and the conditions included should be carefully assessed to determine whether they are performance-related. Where the conditions are general, e.g. funding to "provide   **4.40**

29

meals on wheel" or "dig wells", they are not performance-related and should be recognised when the charity becomes entitled to the grant whether or not the related expenditure has been incurred.

On the other hand, where specific targets are set (e.g. specific number of meals to be delivered) then the grant should be recognised as these targets are met. For performance-related grants, payments under the grant agreement may not coincide with performance and income should be accrued or deferred to match performance and not the pattern of payment of the grant.

Grants specifically for the provision of goods and services to be provided as part of the charitable activities or services to beneficiaries

4.41 Grants derived from the provision of goods or services to beneficiaries are always analysed as incoming resources from charitable activities.

Ancillary trades connected to a primary purpose

4.42 *Ancillary trading* contributes indirectly to the successful furtherance of the charity's charitable purposes. For example, the sale of food and drink in a restaurant/bar by a theatre charity to members of the audience is considered ancillary to the primary purpose of the charity.

The level of annual turnover in trading may have a bearing on whether the trading really is ancillary. This will be a matter of judgement to be considered by the charity trustees.

OTHER INCOMING RESOURCES (A3)

4.43 Other incoming resources will include the receipt of resources that the charity has not been able to analyse within the main incoming resources categories. This will involve a minority of incoming resources and most charities will not have to use this category.

Paragraph 147 of the SORP suggests that the type of income that may fall within this category could include gains on the disposal of an asset held for the charity's own use or a gain on the disposal of a programme-related investment. Programme-related investments (also known as *social investments*) are defined in the Glossary to the SORP as investments:

> "made in pursuit of the organisation's charitable purposes. Although they can generate some financial return (funding may or may not be provided on commercial terms), the primary motivation for making them is not financial but to further the objects of the funding charity. Such investments could include loans to individual beneficiaries (e.g. for housing deposits) or to other charities (for example, in relation to regeneration projects)." (SORP 2005, GL 47)

RESTRICTED AND UNRESTRICTED INCOME AND ENDOWMENT FUNDS

Having analysed the incoming resources into the SOFA head-   **4.44**
ings to which they relate, the charity must then determine whether these funds are restricted, unrestricted or endowment funds. Charities need to account for these individual funds and the accounting records must be kept in such a way that the separate transactions can be identified and reported appropriately. (The accounting for funds is addressed in this text at **Chapter 5, paragraphs 5.76 to 5.78.**)

Restricted funds

Restricted funds are funds that can only be used for a specified   **4.45**
purpose; they have to be separately accounted for in the SOFA. Generally, these funds are raised from an appeal, donations, legacies or bequests and certain grants. The documentation supporting appeals and donation should make it clear whether some or all of the funds raised will be restricted to the specific purpose. Restricted funds may take the form of an asset rather than cash.

Unrestricted funds

Unrestricted funds are funds that are available to the trustees of   **4.46**
the charity to apply for the general purposes of the charity as set out in the governing document, trust deed or constitution. A designated fund is a form of unrestricted fund. *Designated funds*

consist of amounts of unrestricted funds allocated by charity trustees for a specific purpose. The use of these funds is at the discretion of the charity trustees.

4.47 The distinction between restricted and unrestricted income has proved difficult in practice, particularly in the area of grant income. Charities sometimes receive grants as core funding. This funding is generally provided to enable the charity to meet its charitable objects and is not restricted to specific projects or costs and is treated as unrestricted voluntary income. Where the terms attaching to the income define the area for spending more narrowly than the charity's objects, the income should be treated as restricted income.

4.48 Contractual income is common among charities that enter into service level agreements with health authorities, local authorities and Government bodies. These agreements need to be considered on a case-by-case basis to determine whether they should be treated as restricted or unrestricted income from charitable activities. In situations where a funder has a right to recover any surplus, this may indicate that the arrangement is that of a restricted grant. Where the arrangement is that of a contract for services and the charity is providing services in exchange for a fee as part of its charitable objects, this income would be unrestricted.

Endowment funds

4.49 *Endowment funds* are a special type of restricted fund. Where the original terms of the gift require that the capital must be retained intact and not spent, these are *permanent endowment funds*. Generally, these are held on trust as a capital fund and invested to earn a return. The income will usually be unrestricted income unless the terms of the original gift impose restrictions on the use of the income.

Expendable endowment funds are gifts or donations that have been given to a charity to be held as capital, but the trustees of the charity have been given discretionary powers to use the fund as income or to fund certain activities. Where trustees have a power of discretion to convert endowed capital into income the fund is known as an *expendable endowment*.

Endowment funds should be recognised as income in the year in which the charity becomes entitled to the fund and the other criteria for revenue recognition are met. The fund is likely to have revaluation gains or losses as investments have to be stated at market value at the balance sheet date. These gains or losses should be shown as a movement on the fund in the funds section of the SOFA under the heading 'Other Recognised Gains/Losses (D2)'.

AGENCY ARRANGEMENTS AND MONIES HELD IN TRUST

Charities should only recognise income to which they are enti-   **4.50**
tled. This generally means that the charity's trustees must have control over the income and discretion over its use. In situations where a charity acts as an intermediary with little or no control over the application and use of the monies, then these should not be recognised in the SOFA or balance sheet. However, the notes to the financial statements should include details of the monies received and the movement year on year.

Where the charity has control over the funds, e.g. if it can direct how the third party uses the resources, then it should account for the funds as a principal and include the resources in the SOFA and the balance sheet.

RESOURCES EXPENDED (B)

The normal accruals concept applies to the recognition of expen-   **4.51**
diture for charities. Expenditure should only be recognised to the extent that the cost has been incurred in the financial year concerned. Charities should also recognise legal obligations and the associated costs, and are required to provide for future costs where they have a constructive obligation as a result of a past transaction or event (as described by FRS 5 and FRS 12).

Resources expended are split into three key components in the SORP:

- The Cost of Generating Funds (B1)
- The Costs of Charitable Activity (B2)
- The Governance Costs (B3)

In undertaking any activity, support costs may be incurred. Support costs should be allocated to the activity cost category that they support so that the total cost of those activities can be disclosed in the SOFA and further analysis of the activities can be given in the notes to the financial statements. (The allocation of support costs is discussed below in **Chapter 7.**)

THE COST OF GENERATING FUNDS (B1)

4.52   The cost of generating funds relates to the costs associated with generating incoming resources for the charity's work, other than those from undertaking charitable activities, and would include costs such as advertising, and staff and agents' time costs (costs incurred by staff or agents (fundraisers) to scale out gift and donations). The main components of cost within this category are:

- costs of generating voluntary income – costs incurred by a charity or its agent in inducing others to make a gift or donation to it that is voluntary income (see **paragraph 4.58**);
- costs of fundraising trading, including costs of goods sold and other associated costs (see **paragraph 4.59**); and
- costs of managing investments for both capital maintenance and income generation (see **paragraphs 4.60–4.61**).

4.53   It is important to differentiate between the cost of generating funds and the cost of activities in furtherance of a charity's objectives. Certain types of advertising, depending on their target audience and objectives, will be considered to be a cost of generating funds, whereas other forms of advertising will focus more on promoting the charity's objectives.

For example, advertising a 'race night' to raise funds for a charity would be considered to be a cost of generating funds, whereas a newspaper advertisement looking for volunteers to work for the charity would be considered to fall under the category of expenditure to promote a charity's objectives and would be included as charitable activities.

4.54   Costs associated with providing information to potential donors should be treated as costs of generating funds. Particular issues arise where a charity provides information about its activities in the context of a fundraising campaign. Where the information provided is aimed at raising the profile of the charity and attracting funders or donors, the associated costs should be treated as costs of generating funds.

In determining whether the provision of this information falls to be treated as a multipurpose activity (i.e. activity that generates funds and/or is carried out in furtherance of the charity's objectives), a distinction should be drawn between:

> "(a) publicity or information costs involved in raising the profile of a charity which is associated with fundraising (costs of generating funds); and
> (b) publicity or information that is provided in an educational manner in furtherance of the charity's objectives (charitable expenditure)."
>
> (SORP 2005, paragraph 172)

For information to be provided in an educational manner, and **4.55** thereby treated as costs of generating funds, it would be:

> "(a) targeted at beneficiaries or others who can use the information to further the charity's objectives; and
> (b) information or advice on which the recipient can act upon in an informed manner to further the charity's objectives;
> (c) related to other educational activities or objectives undertaken by the charity." (SORP 2005, paragraph 173)

The accounting policy should explain the apportionment of costs **4.56** between activities and any estimation techniques used in determining the allocation. Where any activity is identified as a multipurpose activity and part of the costs are allocated to charitable activities, the policy for the identification of multipurpose activities and the basis on which costs are allocated should be explained in the statement of accounting policies.

The SORP provides that the costs of generating funds should **4.57** not include costs associated with delivering or supporting the provision of goods or services incurred in carrying out the charity's objectives; nor should they include the costs of any subsequent negotiation, monitoring or reporting of contracts or performance-related grants relating to the provision of services (e.g. costs associated with compiling reports on progress to grant providers).

Costs of generating voluntary income (B1a)

4.58   The SORP also requires that, where the costs of raising voluntary income are material, details of the types of activities on which the costs were expended should be shown in the notes to the financial statements. As far as possible, the headings employed should match those used for describing voluntary incoming resources in the SOFA (statement of financial activities). The costs would include agents' costs, where third-party agents are used to raise funds on behalf of the charity. The Glossary to the SORP defines these as:

> "(a)   Such costs will include costs of producing fundraising advertising, marketing and direct mail materials, as well as any remuneration payable to an agent. It will normally include publicity costs but not those used in an educational manner in furtherance of the charity's objects.
> (b)   Such costs will exclude fundraising trading costs."

> (SORP 2005, Appendix 1, GL 13.1)

Fundraising trading: costs of goods sold and other costs (B1b)

4.59   This category should include the costs of trading to raise funds. The cost of goods sold (both bought-in and donated goods for resale) should be disclosed under the overall heading of 'Cost of Generating Funds'. Such costs would include: cost of goods or services sold, staff costs, premises costs, allocated support costs and costs associated with licensing a charity logo (e.g. registering a trademark).

Investment management costs (B1c)

4.60   Investment management fees should also be disclosed separately within the "Costs of Generating Funds" cost category. Investment management fees include the costs of:

(a) portfolio management;
(b) obtaining investment advice;
(c) administration of the investments;
(d) rent collection, property repairs and maintenance charges.

Where these are deducted from income generated from investments by the investment managers the charity should gross up the investment income and show the costs of management separately under this heading.

Investment management fees relating to endowment funds should generally be charged to the endowment fund in the SOFA.

Valuation fees incurred for accounting purposes are normally charged to the governance costs associated with the fund that holds the assets being valued. Costs associated with acquiring and disposing of investments normally form part of the acquisition or disposal cost, and are not normally treated as investment management costs.   **4.61**

CHARITABLE ACTIVITIES (B2)

Resources expended on charitable activities comprise all the resources applied by the charity in undertaking its work to meet its charitable objectives, as opposed to the cost of raising the funds to finance these activities and governance of the charity. Resources expended on charitable activities would include grants payable and costs of activities in furtherance of the charity's objectives. Costs of charitable activities include direct costs of the charitable activities and support costs incurred to deliver those activities.   **4.62**

Information in relation to the amount of support costs allocated to charitable activities should be disclosed in the notes to the financial statements if it is not given in the SOFA. Costs associated with grant making include the grants actually made and the associated support costs. Charities may undertake all of their charitable activities through grant-making activities, while others may undertake activities through a combination of direct service provision and by making grants to third parties to undertake work that contributes to the charity's objectives and programmes. (Grant-making activities are discussed further in **Chapter 6**.)

4.63 Where incoming resources are received by virtue of a restricted grant to provide a specific service, further analysis of charitable activities expenditure may be provided in the notes to the financial statements to demonstrate the link between the incoming resource and the activity that it funds. In this way there will be a clear link showing how the funds received have been applied for the intended purpose.

4.64 Resources expended on charitable activities should be disclosed on the face of the SOFA or in the notes to the financial statements. The disclosures should include:

- an understanding of the nature of the activities undertaken and the resources expended on their provision;
- the amount of support costs allocated to charitable activities;
- where activities are carried out through a combination of direct service or programme activity and grant funding of third parties, the notes to the financial statements should identify the amount of grant-making expenditure and explain the activity funded;
- the split of each activity by how the expenditure has been incurred, i.e. activities undertaken directly, grant and support costs.

4.65 Where grant-making activities are material to the activities of the charity, the disclosures should include an appropriate analysis of the grants which it has made. This should include the following:

- sufficient analysis and explanation to help the reader of the accounts to understand how the grants made relate to the objects of the charity and the policy adopted by the trustees in pursuing these objects;
- identification of the amount of support costs associated with grant-making activities;

- support costs related to grant making including:
  - costs incurred before grants are made as part of the decision-making process;
  - post-grant costs, e.g. monitoring of grants;
  - costs of any central or regional office functions such as general management, payroll administration, budgeting and accounting, information technology, human resources and financing;
- the total amount of grants analysed between grants to individuals and grants to institutions.

SORP 2005 sets out an example table of the breakdown of costs   **4.66**
of charitable activity at Table 5 (reproduced below) (totals should
reconcile with the SOFA and other notes as appropriate).

SOPR 2005 – Table 5. Breakdown of Costs of Charitable Activity				
Activity of Programme	Activities undertaken directly €	Grant funding of activities €	Support cost €	Total €
Activity 1				
Activity 2				
Activity 3				
Total				

GOVERNANCE COSTS (B3)

Governance costs are defined in the SORP as: **4.67**

> "the costs associated with the governance arrangements of the charity which relate to the general running of the charity as opposed to those costs associated with the fundraising or charitable activity..."

(SORP 2005, Appendix, GL 28.1)

These costs generally include all costs associated with the general management and governance of the charity, as opposed to the direct management functions inherent in generating funds and carrying out the charitable activities of the charity. Governance costs will include costs such as audit costs, legal advice, trustee meetings, preparing statutory accounts, etc. Where material, there should also be an apportionment of indirect costs involved in supporting the governance activities (e.g. staff costs may be apportioned on the basis of time spent on governance activities).

4.68 The accounting policies of the charity should explain the nature of costs allocated to the governance category, and an analysis may be provided within the notes to the financial statements of the main items of expenditure in this category.

OTHER RESOURCES EXPENDED (B4)

4.69 Other resources expended will include the payment of any resources that the charity has not been able to analyse within the main resources expended categories. This will apply to a minority of cost types in most charities. Support costs that can be allocated to other activity costs should not be allocated to this category.

TRANSFERS BETWEEN FUNDS (C)

Charities may need to make transfers from one fund to another and these transfers should be shown on the face of the SOFA. This may occur for a number of reasons, such as the transfer from an endowment fund to an unrestricted fund or from a restricted fund (see (a) to (d) below).

4.70 The SORP sets out situations where transfers of funds might occur as follows:

> "(a) when capital funds are released to an income fund from expendable endowments;
> (b) where restricted assets have been released and reallocated to unrestricted income funds;
> (c) to transfer assets from unrestricted income funds to finance a deficit on a restricted fund;
> (d) to transfer the value of fixed assets from restricted to unrestricted funds when the asset has been purchased

> from a restricted fund donation but the asset is held for a general and not a restricted purpose."
>
> (SORP 2005, paragraph 214)

Such transfers should be shown on the face of the SOFA below **4.71** 'Net Incoming/Outgoing Resources Before Transfers' and material transfers should be shown gross and not netted off.

OTHER RECOGNISED GAINS AND LOSSES (D)

Gains and losses arising on disposal, revaluation or impairment **4.72** of fixed assets – whether held for the charity's own use or for investment purposes – will form part of the particular fund in which the investment or other asset concerned is, or was, held at the time of disposal, revaluation or impairment.

Fixed Assets

Impairment losses on assets held for the charity's own use should **4.73** be treated as an additional depreciation charge and included in the relevant resources expended section of the SOFA.

Gains on disposal of fixed assets should be treated as **'Other Incoming Resources'** (A3) and losses on disposal should be treated as an additional depreciation charge and disclosed separately if material.

Revaluation gains and losses (other than impairment losses) should be included under the heading 'Other Gains/Losses' as gains and losses on revaluations of fixed assets (D1).

Investments

The SORP requires that all investment assets (including investments **4.74** and investment properties) should be shown in the balance sheet at market value, or the trustees' best estimates of market value, except for programme-related investments. The SORP requires that any gains or losses on investment assets be included under the heading **'Other Gains/Losses'** as gains and losses on revaluation and disposal of investment assets (D2). Realised gains and losses in unincorporated charities may be combined on the SOFA. Charitable companies will have to comply with the provisions of the Companies

Acts and show realised gains and losses in the profit and loss account and unrealised gains and losses in the STRGL.

4.75 Programme-related assets should be included in the balance sheet at the amount invested less any impairment (in the case of equity or loans) and any amounts repaid in the case of loans. Impairments should be charged to resources expended on charitable activities (B2). Gains made on the disposal of a programme-related investment should be offset first against any previous impairment or included as a gain on disposal of a fixed asset for the charity's own use under **'Other Incoming Resources'** (A3).

Actuarial gains and losses on defined benefit schemes

4.76 Actuarial gains and losses on defined benefit pension schemes should be separately disclosed under the heading **'Other Gains/ Losses'** as actuarial gains/losses on defined benefit pension schemes (D3).

RECONCILIATION OF FUNDS

Closing Position

4.77 In the SOFA (statement of financial activities), the funds of the charity will be reconciled under each of the three headings, restricted, unrestricted and endowment funds. The net movement in funds represents the increase or decrease in available resources. The closing balance represents the funds carried forward to the next period.

Deferred Income

4.78 In certain scenarios, a charity may have received voluntary income in advance of the balance sheet date for which specific terms have been imposed by the funding organisation which have not yet been met at the balance sheet date. Such incoming resources should not be recognised in the SOFA until the specified conditions have been satisfied. Therefore, such income is treated as deferred income in the Balance Sheet and will not therefore form part of the reconciliation of funds on the SOFA.

Chapter 5

BALANCE SHEET

INTRODUCTION

The balance sheet of a charity is a snapshot at a point in time of its assets and liabilities at that date and how assets are split between the different funds available to the charity. **5.1**

The balance sheet may not include all assets of the charity. For example, heritage assets may not be included, but information on these assets should be included in the notes to the financial statements in accordance with FRS 30 – Heritage Assets.

Assets included in the balance sheet may be included at historic cost and the accounting policy in respect of fixed assets should clearly state whether they are carried at cost or valuation.

The objective of the balance sheet is to show the resources of the charity at a particular date and to clearly indicate whether these resources are freely available (unrestricted) for use in further- ance of the charity's objectives or whether restricted in use. The reserves policy of the charity should clearly state the activity for which these reserves are held. The SORP requires trustees to set out in the Trustees' Report the activity and planned use of funds. Irish charities adopting the SORP should include these details in the Trustees'/Directors' Report. **5.2**

STRUCTURE OF THE BALANCE SHEET

The SORP sets out at 'Table 7' the structure to be adopted in respect of the balance sheet, and this is reproduced below. (**Note:** references in this chapter to the different balance sheet categories will include, where appropriate, the reference num- bers shown in this table.) **5.3**

SORP 2005 – Table 7. Balance Sheet

		Total Funds €	Prior Year Funds €	SORP Reference
A	**Fixed assets:**			
A1	Intangible assets			252
A2	Tangible assets			253 to 278
A3	Heritage assets			279 to 294
A4	Investments:			
A4a	Investments			295 to 307
A4b	Programme related investments			308 to 312
	Total fixed assets			
B	**Current assets**			313 to 316
B1	Stocks and work-in-progress			
B2	Debtors			314
B3	Investments			316
B4	Cash at bank and in hand			
	Total current assets			
C	**Liabilities**			
C1	Creditors: amounts falling due within one year			317 to 320
	Net current assets or liabilities			
	Total assets less current liabilities			
C2	Creditors: amounts falling due after more than one year			317 to 320
C3	Provisions for liabilities and charges			321 to 329
	Net assets or liabilities excluding pension asset or liability			
D	**Defined benefit pension scheme asset or liability**			330 to 332
	Net assets or liabilities including pension asset or liability			

SORP 2005 – Table 7. Balance Sheet – *cont.*

E	The funds of the charity			
E1	Endowment funds			
E2	Restricted income funds			
E3	Unrestricted income funds			
E3a	Share capital			333
E3b	Unrestricted income funds			
E3c	Revaluation reserve			334
	Unrestricted income funds excluding pension asset/liability			
E3d	Pension reserve			335
	Total unrestricted funds			
	Total charity funds			

The paragraphs that follow in this chapter provide detail and discussion of each of the main headings in the balance sheet. The notes to the financial statements should provide additional information on each of the material items in the balance sheet. The information provided should be such as to enable the reader to gain a proper appreciation of the nature and spread of the assets and liabilities.   5.4

INTANGIBLE FIXED ASSETS (A1)

An intangible fixed asset is a non-financial fixed asset that does not have physical substance, but is separately identifiable and is controlled by the charity. These assets should be recognised in accordance with FRS10 – Goodwill and Intangible Assets.   5.5

Intangible assets, such as goodwill, tend to be rare in the charity sector. Some charities may have intangible assets relating to intellectual property or patents. An internally developed intangible asset may be capitalised only if it has a readily ascertainable market value (per FRS 10, paragraph 14).   5.6

In practice, hardly any intangible assets will have a readily ascertainable market value and those that do are, in any case, unlikely to be developed internally.   5.7

In all other cases, the costs of developing intangible assets must be written off as incurred. Where intangible assets are acquired, they should be capitalised at cost. Intangible fixed assets should be amortised over their useful life, normally not exceeding 20 years. If intangible fixed assets are not amortised, an annual impairment review must be performed.

TANGIBLE FIXED ASSETS (A2)

5.8 The accounting treatment and disclosure of the standard categories of tangible fixed assets is set out in Financial Reporting Standard 15 – Tangible Fixed Assets (FRS 15). For those charities that wish to adopt the SORP, paragraphs 253 to 294 of the SORP set out the general rules for accounting for tangible fixed assets by charities. The SORP distinguishes between those held for charity use, those held as investments and those held as heritage assets.

5.9 Fixed assets will normally comprise the buildings and equipment used by the charity. Generally, charities will set a threshold or value for items to be treated as fixed assets. Items below this threshold will be included as expenditure in the income and expenditure account or SOFA (statement of financial activities). There is no set limit on the threshold to be chosen and it will depend on the circumstances of each individual charity.

5.10 A fixed asset register should be maintained providing a detailed inventory of all assets owned by the charity, their age, original cost, revaluation amount (if applicable), depreciation rate and accumulated balance, and estimated useful life.

5.11 The general rule for the inclusion of tangible fixed assets is that they should initially be included at cost of acquisition including any costs of bringing the assets into working condition for their intended use. FRS 15 prescribes that tangible fixed assets (other than investments):

(a) should be capitalised on initial recognition and included in the balance sheet at cost or valuation;
(b) may be periodically revalued;
(c) all subsequent expenditure which enhances the performance of the asset should be capitalised.

(SORP 2005, paragraph 253)

Initial recognition and valuation

All tangible fixed assets should be initially recorded in the bal-   **5.12**
ance sheet using one of the following bases as set out in SORP
2005, paragraph 255:

(a) the cost of acquisition including those costs that are
directly attributable to bringing the assets into working
condition for their intended use;

(b) if a functional fixed asset (an asset which is used for charitable purposes) is acquired in full or in part from the proceeds of a grant it should be included at its full acquisition
cost without netting off the grant proceeds;

(c) where functional fixed assets have been donated, they
should be included in the balance sheet at their current
value at the date of the gift and in the SOFA as voluntary
income. In the case of charities that are companies, the
donated asset would be recognised in the STRGL;

(d) where functional fixed assets are capitalised some time after
being acquired they should be included at original cost or at
the value at which the gift was recorded (less any depreciation). If neither of these amounts is available, a reasonable
estimate of the asset's cost or current value to the charity
should be used. Such a valuation will be regarded as the
asset's initial carrying amount and will not be regarded as a
revaluation. Current value will be either replacement cost
existing use or market value existing use. This valuation
would normally be arrived at by professional valuers. The
valuation should take into account the location of the assets
and whether the asset is still required by the charity in carrying out its charitable activities.

Revaluation of fixed assets

FRS 15 does not require a charity to revalue its assets unless it   **5.13**
specifically adopts such an accounting policy from the outset. If
a policy of revaluation is adopted, the policy will have to be
applied to the entire class of assets – this could prove to be an
extensive and laborious task, which would have to be repeated
indefinitely at least every three to five years.

However, if a revaluation policy is adopted, the demands placed
on charities in respect of revaluations by the SORP are not as
challenging as other companies for the following reasons:

(a) the SORP (at paragraph 265) states that it is acceptable to carry out a rolling valuation over a five-year period;

(b) an independent formal professional valuation is not mandatory – a valuation may be obtained from a suitably qualified person who could be a trustee or an employee.

5.14 However, it should be noted that the SORP is not mandatory for adoption by charities in Ireland. Charities that are companies, and other charities whose financial statements are required to give a true and fair view, will need to follow the requirements of FRS 15 in relation to revaluations of fixed assets.

5.15 The initial valuation of an asset when it is donated, or where it is capitalised as a result of a change in accounting policy, will not be regarded as a revaluation, and will not require a revaluation of the entire class of assets.

Subsequent expenditure

5.16 Subsequent expenditure on fixed assets should be capitalised, where the performance of the asset is enhanced, rather than just maintained. Though the SORP does not specifically address this issue, the general rule in relation to subsequent expenditure on fixed assets is that it should be written off as incurred. Such expenditure is generally of a repairs and maintenance nature and does not improve the asset beyond the standard of performance previously expected of it.

There are, however, three exceptions to this general rule:

1. where the subsequent expenditure provides an enhancement of the economic benefits of the asset in excess of the previously assessed performance, e.g. upgrading machine parts to achieve substantial improvement in quality of output;

2. where a component of an asset that has been treated separately for depreciation purposes and depreciated over its individual useful economic life, is replaced or restored, e.g. a lift within a charity's building;

3. where the subsequent expenditure relates to a major inspection or overhaul of the fixed asset and restores the economic benefits of the asset that have been used up by the entity and that have already been reflected in the

depreciation charge, e.g. expenditure that maintains the structural integrity of the underlying assets, e.g. where a major overhaul of an asset is required by law.

Other matters of relevance to charities

Certain aspects of the accounting standards on fixed assets may have specific relevance to charities, including: **5.17**

- varying uses for fixed assets, particularly land and buildings
- varying asset lives for different components of the same assets
- impairment of fixed assets
- grant funding of fixed assets
- depreciation

These are discussed individually below.

Varying uses for fixed assets, particularly land and buildings

Certain charities may use land and buildings partly for their own use and partly for investment purposes (i.e. when they have a portion of the building leased out). The accounting treatment for such buildings should reflect the primary purpose of holding them: if a large part of the building is leased out on a long-term lease, the primary purpose of holding that asset would appear to be similar in nature to an investment asset and vice versa. Where the own use part of the building and the investment part are both significant and are clearly distinguishable they should be apportioned and analysed in the balance sheet between functional and investment assets. **5.18**

Varying asset lives for different components of the same assets

A charity shop, which may be expanding its range of products, may incur costs in fitting out the new shop. The equipment used in fit-out is likely to have a useful life, which may be shorter than the useful life attributed to the building in which the shop operates. In this scenario, it would not be appropriate to write off the cost of fit-out in Year 1, but rather to depreciate over the period of time in which the equipment and fittings are expected to **5.19** contribute to the revenue generating activities of the shop. This may be, say, five years, whereas the building itself may be depreciated over, say, 50 years.

Thus, where any fixed asset for charity use comprises two or more components and these can be separately identified into distinguishable components, each component should be accounted for as a separate asset and depreciated over its useful life.

Impairment of fixed assets

5.20   Where the recoverable amount of a tangible fixed asset decreases below the net book value at which it is recorded, an impairment has occurred and FRS 11 – Impairment of Fixed Assets and Goodwill requires that the asset be written down to its recoverable amount.

Situations that may trigger an impairment include:

- physical deterioration or obsolescence;
- social demographic or environmental changes resulting in a reduction in the beneficiaries of a particular charity;
- changes in laws or regulations impacting on a charity;
- loss of key employees associated with a particular aspect of a charity; or
- losses on charitable activities using fixed assets to generate income.

5.21   The accounting standard (FRS 11) is written from the perspective of commercial enterprises where fixed assets are employed to generate cash flows for the business. Where fixed assets are not held for the purpose of generating cash flows (such as certain assets held by charities) the value to such organisations of fixed assets acquired for the purpose of carrying out their charitable activities cannot meaningfully be measured in terms of cash flow, because the benefits that derive from their use are not financial. The normal accounting treatment of these assets is that they are depreciated systematically over their estimated useful lives, that is, as they wear out or as the benefits are otherwise consumed.

5.22   The accounting standard refers briefly to this issue and explains that it may not be appropriate to write down such assets to their recoverable amount and that "*an alternative measure of its*

service potential may be more relevant" (FRS 11, paragraph 20).
In practice, an impairment of an asset employed in a non-cash
generating activity is likely to arise only where the asset suffers
impairment in a physical sense, for example, where the asset is
physically damaged, where it is no longer in use or use of the
asset has reduced significantly, or where the quality of service
that it provides has deteriorated. As long as such assets continue to provide the anticipated benefits to the charity, the
consumption of such benefits will be reflected in regular depreciation charges.

Grant funding of fixed assets

There is considerable debate as to the appropriate treatment of   **5.23**
capital grants in the case of charities and other public benefit
entities. The Accounting Standards Board (ASB) in its *Interpretation for Public Benefit Entities of the Statement of Principles*
('Interpretation') states that, where a capital grant is not a capital
contribution and it results in an increase in the net assets, then it
should be recognised as a gain. This treatment would result in
the grant being recognised as income. It corresponds with the
treatment set out in SORP 2005.

The practice adopted by charities in the Republic of Ireland var-   **5.24**
ies. Many adopt the provisions of Statement of Accounting
Practice (SSAP) No. 4 – Accounting for Grants. In those cases the
grant is accounted for as a deferred credit and released to income
as the related asset is depreciated.

Under SORP 2005, where a tangible asset is funded by way of   **5.25**
capital grant, this funding is deemed to be a restricted fund
and is recognised in the SOFA when the charity is entitled to
the grant. In the case of such assets, grants are not netted against
the cost of the asset. The full cost of the asset should be shown
on the balance sheet under fixed assets and the depreciation for
the year will be shown as a movement on the restricted fund
created by receipt of the grant. The balance at the end of each
financial year which is carried forward as a restricted fund will
then match the net book value of the fixed asset.

In all cases, the assets should be included at full cost or current   **5.26**
value in the balance sheet and depreciated. The accounting

policy should clearly state the accounting policy that has been adopted, and additional information to assist the user of the financial statements should be given in the notes to the financial statements.

Depreciation

5.27   Tangible fixed assets held for use should be depreciated at rates appropriate to their useful economic life.

There are three exceptions to charging depreciation, which are as follows:

1. where the asset is freehold land which is considered to have an indefinite useful life;
2. where both the depreciation charge and the accumulated depreciation are not material (e.g. the asset has a very long useful life);
3. where the assets are heritage assets and have not been included on the balance sheet.

HERITAGE ASSETS

5.28   Most tangible fixed assets held by charities are held for their own use. Some charities also hold historic or inalienable assets referred to as *heritage assets*, which are dealt with in FRS 30 – Heritage Assets (issued on 19 June 2009 and effective for accounting periods commencing on or after 1 April 2010). Examples of such assets are:

- ancient monuments,
- historic buildings,
- collections of artistic or scientific works.

5.29   The Accounting Standards Board issued FRS 30 – Heritage Assets to improve the accounting and reporting by entities of heritage assets held. The objective of FRS 30 is to ensure that:

"(i) enhanced disclosures apply to all heritage assets, regardless of whether they are reported in the balance sheet; and

(ii) where information is available on cost or value, heritage assets are reported in the balance sheet".

A *heritage asset* is defined in FRS 30 as: **5.30**

"A tangible asset with historical, artistic, scientific, technological, geophysical or environmental qualities that is held and maintained principally for its contribution to knowledge and culture."

Heritage assets qualify as assets because they have a specific   **5.31**
use, i.e. for educational or cultural purposes, and are central to the operation of many entities such as museums and galleries. FRS 30 (in Appendix I) explains that works of art and historic assets **not** maintained for their contribution to knowledge and culture are *excluded* from the definition of heritage assets. Assets held by a charity, but not for preservation or cultural purposes, cannot be regarded as heritage assets as their preservation may not be the primary purpose of the charity. Examples of these assets might include historic churches, cathedrals and abbeys.

The accounting standard requires charities, whose accounts are   **5.32**
intended to give a true and fair view, to determine the cost or value of heritage assets and include them as a separate line item in the balance sheet. Where the cost or value of the heritage asset cannot be obtained at a cost commensurate with the benefits to users of the financial statements, enhanced disclosures in respect of these assets are required. The disclosure requirements in respect of heritage assets can be summarised as follows:

General disclosures

The following general disclosures should be provided in the financial statements:
- the nature and scale of the charity's heritage assets;
- the accounting policy adopted in respect of heritage assets and the measurement bases used to determine cost or valuation; and
- the policy for acquisition, preservation, maintenance and disposal of heritage assets.

Disclosures in respect of assets recognised

Where heritage assets have been recognised, the following disclosures should be provided:
- the carrying amount at opening and closing balance sheet date should be disclosed;
- information about the valuations, e.g. method used, date of valuation, internal or external valuers; and
- a five-year summary showing cost of acquisition, value of donated assets, carrying value, disposal proceeds and any impairment recognised in the period.

Disclosures in respect of assets not recognised

In respect of heritage assets not included in the balance sheet, the reasons why they are not included, the nature of those assets and the scale and importance of those assets to the charity should be stated.

5.33 FRS 30 provides that the recognition and measurement of heritage assets should follow the requirements of FRS 15 as supplemented by FRS 30, which provides for valuations to be made by any method that is appropriate and relevant. To encourage a valuation approach, FRS 30 permits entities to use internal valuations without the requirement for a full valuation every five years.

5.34 Appendix II of FRS 30 sets out illustrative examples of the additional disclosures for heritage assets.

INVESTMENT ASSETS

5.35 Investment assets (including investments and investment properties, and cash held for investment) need to be classified as a separate category within fixed assets and should be shown at market value or the trustees' best estimate of market value, except for programme-related investments. Programme-related investments are also known as social investments and are made directly in pursuit of the charity's objectives. Programme-related assets should be included in the balance sheet at the amount invested, less any impairment (in the case of equity or loans) and any amounts repaid in the case of loans.

Investment assets should not be depreciated. All changes in value in the year, whether realised or not, should be reported in the 'Gains and Losses on Investment Assets' section of the SOFA (D2). **5.36**

The charity's powers of investment should be set out in its governing document. Where investment managers are engaged to manage investments, a clear, written mandate should be given to the investment managers and this should be regularly reviewed and updated. **5.37**

The SORP requires investment assets to be analysed in the notes to the financial statements between:

(a) investments held primarily to provide an investment return for the charity; and
(b) programme-related investments that the charity makes as part of its charitable activities.

Information on the valuation methods, names and qualifications of the valuers of non-quoted investments should also be disclosed. Charity trustees need to exercise care and due diligence in making investments and need to understand fully the nature and risks associated with all investments, particularly non-quoted (alternate investments). **5.38**

The opening and closing values of investments, together with movements during the year (additions, disposals, and impairments) should be disclosed, together with an analysis of the total value of investments at year end by class of investment. **5.39**

If any particular investment is considered material in the context of the investment portfolio, additional information should be included in the notes to the financial statements. The notes to the financial statements should also indicate the value of investments held in each category of fund. **5.40**

Presentation and Disclosure

Charities should adopt a traditional columnar approach to presenting their assets in the notes to the financial statements. Essentially, the notes to the financial statements need to ensure that all separate categories are appropriately disclosed with all movements during the year fully reflected as follows: **5.41**

Notes to the financial statements

	Freehold Land & Buildings €	Leasehold Land & Buildings €	Motor Vehicles €	Fixtures and Fittings €	Total €	Heritage Assets* €
Asset at cost, valuation or revalued amount At beginning of year						
Additions						
Disposals						
Revaluations						
Transfers						
At end of year						
Accumulated depreciation and impairment provisions At beginning of year						
Disposals						
Revaluations						
Charge for the year						
Impairment charges						
Transfers						
At end of year						
Net Book Value – end of year						
Net Book Value – beginning of year						
* The SORP shows heritage assets separately in the balance sheet.						

	Investment Assets €
Carrying value at beginning of year/initial recognition	Market Value
Add: Additions to investments at cost	
Less: Disposals at carrying value	
Add/Deduct: Net gain/(loss) on revaluation	
Carrying value at the end of the year	Market Value

Accounting policy for fixed assets

The accounting policy for fixed assets should provide the fol-   **5.42**
lowing information:

(a) whether the asset is accounted for at cost, valuation or revalued amount and the method of valuation, if appropriate;
(b) whether heritage assets are capitalised, and the basis of valuation if they are capitalised. If they are not capitalised, the reason for non-capitalisation should be disclosed;
(c) the basis of depreciation and the rates/useful lives of fixed assets; and
(d) the policy in relation to impairment reviews including the methods used in arriving at net realisable value (NRV) or value in use (VIU).

Designated funds for fixed assets

Fixed assets frequently represent a significant portion of the   **5.43**
assets of a charity. In order to provide users of the financial
statements with useful information in relation to the total
funds position of the charity, it would be useful if charities
identified a portion of its reserves as a designated fund for
fixed assets.

The ASB interpretation suggests that only designations made   **5.44**
as a result of a trust or other legal requirements should be
shown on the balance sheet. Other designations made by management reflecting the future intentions should be shown in the
notes to the financial statements or in the accompanying
information.

CURRENT ASSETS (B)

5.45 Current assets (other than current asset investments) should be recognised at the lower of cost and net realisable value. Current assets comprise:

- Stocks and work-in-progress (B1);
- debtors (B2);
- investments (B3); and
- Cash at bank and in hand (B4).

5.46 Where there are debtors that do not fit into the categories set out in the SORP, the headings should be adapted as appropriate, namely:

- Trade debtors;
- Amounts falling due from subsidiary and associated undertakings;
- Other debtors;
- Prepayments and accrued income.

Long-term debtors should be shown separately in the balance sheet, where material. Investment assets held as current assets should be disclosed in the same way as investments held as fixed assets.

CURRENT LIABILITIES (C)

5.47 Current liabilities comprise amounts falling due within one year (C1) and should be recognised at their settlement value. In the case of provisions, an estimate may be included based on the amount at which a charity may reasonably expect to settle the obligation or transfer it to a third party.

5.48 Where creditors do not fit into the categories set out in the SORP, which are:

- loans and overdrafts,
- trade creditors,
- amounts due to subsidiary and associated undertakings,
- other creditors,

- accruals, and
- deferred income

the headings may be adapted to suit the charity's circumstances. The totals for long- and short-term creditors should be analysed and totalled over the headings set out above.

Where a charity is acting as an intermediary agent (as opposed   **5.49** to a custodian trustee) for another organisation, any assets held and the associated liabilities should be separately disclosed in the notes to the financial statements but should not be included in the balance sheet.

Where the charity is acting as an intermediary principal, the assets and associated liabilities should be disclosed and also included in the balance sheet.

LONG-TERM CREDITORS (C2)

Long-term creditors comprise amounts falling due after more   **5.50** than one year (C2). Where long-term liabilities include loan liabilities, details of any mortgages or charges given as security for the loan must be disclosed in the notes to the financial statements. The disclosure should provide details of the assets that are subject to mortgage or charge, and the amount of the loan or liability and its proportion to the value of the assets mortgaged or charged.

PROVISIONS FOR LIABILITIES AND CHARGES (C3)

The general principles for recognition of a provision in the finan-   **5.51** cial statements are set out in FRS 12. For those charities that wish to adopt the SORP, the general rules for accounting for provisions for liabilities and charges are set out at paragraphs 321 to 329.

The SORP also distinguishes between provisions and unrestricted funds that have been earmarked for a specific purpose (designated funds). No provision is recognised for funds designated for future use, for example where reserves are designated for a future building project.

5.52   A *provision* is defined by FRS 12 as a liability of uncertain timing or amount. Only liabilities that exist at the balance sheet date can be recognised.

Recognition criteria for provisions

5.53   FRS 12 prescribes that a provision should be recognised when the following three criteria are satisfied:

1. the charity has a present obligation (either legal or constructive) arising as a result of a past event;
2. it is probable that a transfer of economic benefits will be required to settle the obligation; and
3. a reliable estimate of the obligation can be made.

5.54   The amount actually recognised as a liability should be the best estimate of the expenditure required to settle the obligation at the balance sheet date. When calculating the amount of the liability to be recognised, consideration should be given to the timing of the cash flows and future events or uncertainties that may impact on the amount required to settle the liability. Where a provision is to be paid over a period of time, the charity should use an appropriate discount rate, and the expected cash flows required to settle the obligation should be discounted to their present value. An appropriate discount rate would usually be either the cost of borrowing or the interest rate applicable to investments. The liability recognised should be reviewed at each balance sheet date to ensure that it is still appropriate. Where a change in circumstances results in a lower liability, the element of the liability no longer representing the obligation should be credited to the expense line in the SOFA, where it was first recorded as an expense.

Specific examples where provisions can or cannot be recognised

5.55   FRS 12 addresses a number of specific examples of where provisions can or cannot be recognised in the financial statements. A number of these may have relevance to a charity's set of accounts.

Future Operating Losses

There is a general rule in FRS 12 that provisions cannot be recognised for future operating losses. Thus, if a charity is forecasting a deficit for the coming year, due to a known shortfall in funding from a funding agency, it would not be appropriate for that charity to provide for those losses in advance in the current year financial statements. The reason for this is that the 'future operating losses' do not derive from a past event.

Restructuring/Redundancy provisions

Under FRS 12, a provision is only allowed for restructuring or redundancy costs if there is an obligating event at the balance sheet date. For a constructive obligation to arise, certain evidence is required, including a detailed formal plan, which has been both approved by the trustees/board of directors and communicated to the third parties impacted prior to the balance sheet date. This plan would need to identify:

- the element of the charity's activities impacted;
- the locations affected;
- the function and number of employees impacted;
- the associated costs (redundancy costs, etc.); and
- the timing of implementation.

Onerous contracts

Where a charity has a contract that is onerous, FRS 12 requires that a provision be made for the present obligation that arises under that contract.

For example, if a charity which provided night centre accommodation closed down one of its shelters and terminated the lease on the premises five years earlier than the lease was due to expire, the charity will need to provide for the remaining obligation that arises under the lease contract.

Presentation and disclosure

Provisions should be analysed in the balance sheet between liabilities due in less than one year and liabilities due after more than one year. For each provision, movements on the provision during the year should be shown in the following format: **5.56**

Opening balance at beginning of period	X
Additional provisions made in period (including increases to existing provisions)	X
Amounts utilised/charged against provision in period	(X)
Unused amounts reversed in period	(X)
Increase/decrease in provision arising from change in discount rate effect	X
Closing balance at period end	X

5.57 In addition to the above, FRS 12 requires narrative disclosures to be provided detailing the nature of the obligation, expected timing of any transfers of economic benefits, an indication of the uncertainties surrounding the amount or timing of cash flows and the amount of any expected reimbursement.

5.58 In extremely rare cases, disclosure need not be given if it can be expected to prejudice seriously the position of the entity in a dispute with other parties.

Contingent liabilities

5.59 A *contingent liability* is either:

(a) a possible obligation arising from past events whose existence will be confirmed only by the occurrence of one or more uncertain future events not wholly within the entity's control; or

(b) a present obligation arising from past events that is not recognised because it is not probable that a transfer of economic benefits will be made or because it cannot be measured with sufficient reliability.

5.60 Contingent liabilities should not be provided for, but should be disclosed unless remote. FRS 12 contains extensive disclosure requirements for contingent liabilities.

For each class of contingent liability, the charity must disclose:

(a) a best estimate of its financial effect (either the most likely outcome or weighted average depending on facts and circumstances);

(b) an indication of the uncertainties relating to the amount or timing of any outflow;

(c) the possibility of any reimbursement;

(d) its legal nature; and

(e) whether any valuable security has been provided by the charity in connection with the liability.

Charities should continually reassess contingent liabilities to determine if the conditions giving rise to the contingent liability have changed and whether there is a need to recognise a liability.

Contingent assets

Contingent assets are never recognised as a result of the degree **5.61** of certainty that has to exist before an entity can recognise an asset in its balance sheet. (There must be evidence that an asset exists and the control of access to future benefits is controlled by the charity.) They are required to be disclosed by FRS 12, but only where an inflow of economic benefit is probable. Where an inflow of economic benefit is probable, the charity must disclose a brief description of the nature of the contingent assets at the balance sheet date and, where practicable, an estimate of their financial effect.

Because of the higher degree of certainty required before a contingent asset is disclosed, it is important that disclosures of contingent assets avoid giving a misleading indication of the likelihood of benefits arising. Charities should continually reassess contingent assets to determine if the conditions giving rise to the contingent asset have changed and whether there is a need to recognise an asset.

Where material contingent assets and liabilities exist, the fol- **5.62** lowing should be disclosed in the notes to the financial statements:

- the nature of each contingency;
- the uncertainties that are expected to affect the outcome;
- a prudent estimate of the financial effect where an amount has not been accrued or an explanation as to why it is not practicable to make such an estimate;
- where there is more than one contingent asset or liability and they are sufficiently similar in nature they should be grouped together as one class and disclosed in a single statement.

Commitments

5.63   Particulars of all material commitments that have not been charged in the financial statements should be disclosed.

5.64   The notes to the financial statements should distinguish between those commitments included in the balance sheet as commitments and those that are intentions to spend and are not recognised at the balance sheet date. The following should be disclosed in respect of commitments:

- the reason for the commitments, giving separate disclosure for material projects;
- the total amount of the commitments, including amounts already charged in the accounts;
- the amount of commitments outstanding at the start of the year;
- any amounts charged in the SOFA during the year;
- any amounts released during the year due to a change in the value of the commitments;
- the amount of commitments outstanding at the year end and an indication as to how much is payable within one year and over one year.

The portion of unrestricted funds that have been set aside to meet the commitments should be designated as such in the notes to the financial statements.

DEFINED BENEFIT PENSION SCHEME ASSET OR LIABILITY (D)

5.65   FRS 17 – Retirement Benefits was published in November 2000 and had a long implementation period. Full adoption of the standard was not required until accounting periods commencing on or after 1 January 2005. FRS 17 applies to all types of benefits that an employer provides to employees when they have completed their service with the entity. While FRS 17 deals primarily with pension benefits, other benefits such as health benefits provided to employees post retirement are also covered by the standard.

5.66   Where a charity participates in a multi-employer scheme, in some cases the individual participating entities will treat the scheme as a defined contribution scheme. For **defined contribution** schemes, the accounting is straightforward and the charge for the period is equal to the contributions payable to the scheme for the period. Where a charity has established that the employer's share of underlying assets and liabilities cannot be identified on a consistent and reasonable manner, this fact should be disclosed. Any available information about the existence of the surplus or deficit in the scheme and the implications of that surplus or deficit should be disclosed with a brief explanation of the general circumstances giving rise to this position.

The accounting for **defined benefit** schemes is more complex. **5.67** Pension scheme assets should be measured at fair value. For quoted investments, this is bid market value; for properties it is open market value. Liabilities should be measured on an actuarial basis, using the projected unit method. The accounting standard requires that pension liabilities should be discounted using the current rate of return on an AA-rated corporate bond of equivalent currency and term to the scheme liabilities. AA-rated bonds or indices alone cannot be relied upon as the sole source for setting a discount rate for a typical plan. This is because AA-rated bonds are generally much shorter in duration than the liabilities of Irish pension plans. In such cases, an entity estimates the discount rate for longer maturities by extrapolating current market rates for AA bonds along the yield curve (possibly with reference to government bonds). In determining the bond yield the Iboxx (or equivalent) from corporate bond indices 'outliers' within these indices should be excluded.

A full actuarial valuation of the scheme (being the difference **5.68** between the scheme assets and liabilities) should be carried out at least every three years (by an independent qualified actuary) with an annual actuarial review to reflect current conditions. Where death-in-service and incapacity benefits are not fully insured, they should be included in the valuation of liabilities.

The surplus or deficit of the scheme should be recognised in the **5.69** balance sheet and shown separately after all other assets and liabilities. The surplus or deficit shown should be shown as accruing to unrestricted reserves in the charity's balance sheet. A surplus or deficit on the pension scheme should only be shown as accruing to a restricted fund where it can be demonstrated that only that fund will benefit from any surplus and, in the event of a deficit, that fund will have to make good the deficit. When considering the appropriateness of the going concern concept, charity trustees and directors need to consider the cash flow effects of the agreed pension contributions to defined benefit pension schemes.

5.70 The use of market values in the balance sheet will often give rise to significant volatility in the amounts reported as pension assets or liabilities. In the case of charities, changes in market values will be recognised in the SOFA as set out above in **Chapter 4, paragraph 4.76**.

5.71 Charities not adopting the SORP should comply with FRS 17 and include current service costs, past service costs, gains/losses or curtailments and finance costs in the income and expenditure account. Actuarial gains and losses should be reported in the Statement of Recognised Gains and Losses (STRGL).

Presentation and disclosure

5.72 The disclosure requirements for defined benefit pension schemes are set out in FRS 17 and are summarised below.

Defined contribution schemes

Where a defined contribution scheme is operated by the charity, the following information should be disclosed:

(a) the nature of the scheme;
(b) the costs of the scheme for the period under review; and
(c) the amount of any unpaid or prepaid contributions at the end of the period.

Defined benefit schemes

The disclosure requirements under FRS 17 (paragraphs 76–82) are detailed and charities should refer to the main text to ensure compliance. The disclosure requirements are extensive and were revised in December 2006. Key disclosure requirements include:

(a) the principal assumptions underlying the scheme;

(b) a reconciliation of the opening and closing balances of the fair value of scheme assets and the opening and closing balances of scheme liabilities showing effects during the period that give rise to the movement in the opening and closing balances;

(c) for each major category of scheme assets the percentage or the amount that each major category constitutes of the fair value of the total scheme assets;

(d) a narrative description of the basis used to determine the overall expected rate of return on assets; and

(e) the amounts for the current and previous four periods of the present value of the scheme liabilities, the fair value of the scheme assets and the surplus or deficit in the scheme.

The paragraphs below set out the disclosures required in respect   **5.73** of defined benefit pension schemes.

Accounting policy disclosure: example

The accounting policy for defined benefit pension schemes   **5.74** should be disclosed. An example disclosure is given below.

RETIREMENT BENEFITS

Defined benefit pension scheme assets are measured at fair value. Defined benefit pension scheme liabilities are measured on an actuarial basis using the projected unit method. The excess of scheme liabilities over scheme assets is presented on the balance sheet as a liability. The defined benefit pension charge to operating profit comprises the current service cost and past service costs. The excess of the expected return on scheme assets over the interest cost on the scheme liabilities is presented in the profit and loss account as other finance income. Actuarial gains and losses arising from changes in actuarial assumptions and from experience surpluses and deficits are recognised in the statement of total recognised gains and losses for the year in which they occur.

The defined contribution pension charge to operating profit comprises the contribution payable to the scheme for the year.

Notes to the financial statements

5.75   The following information should be given in the notes to the financial statements:

EXAMPLE – RETIREMENT BENEFITS

The charity operates a defined benefit pension scheme with assets held in a separately administered fund. The scheme provides retirement benefits on the basis of members' final salary. The contributions are determined by a qualified actuary on the basis of triennial valuations using the projected unit method. On 1 January 2006 the scheme was closed to new entrants. As this scheme is closed it has an age profile that is rising and therefore under the projected unit method the current service cost will increase as the members of the scheme approach retirement. At the same time the charity established a defined contribution scheme to provide benefits to new employees. Contributions made to the defined contribution scheme during the year amounted to €58,000 (2008: €46,000). There were no contributions in relation to either scheme payable at the year-end (2008: Nil). The most recent valuation for funding purposes was carried out by a qualified independent actuary as at 30 June 2009 and is available for inspection by the scheme members but not for public inspection.

A full actuarial valuation, on which the amounts recognised in the financial statements are based, was carried out at 30 June 2009.

The amounts recognised in the balance sheet are as follows:

	2009 €'000	2008 €'000
Present value of scheme liabilities	(7,176)	(7,131)
Fair value of scheme assets	7,073	7,012
Pension Liability	(103)	(119)
Related deferred tax asset	13	15
Net pension liability	(90)	(104)

Retirement benefits – *cont.*	2009 €'000	2008 €'000
The amounts recognised in the profit and loss account are as follows:		
Interest cost	421	314
Expected return on scheme assets	(498)	(433)
Other finance income	(77)	(119)
Current service cost – included in other operating costs	311	300
	234	181

In the case of charities that are companies the amounts recognised in the Statement of Total Recognised Gains and Losses are as follows:

	2009 €'000	2008 €'000
Actual less expected return on scheme assets	(751)	139
Experience losses on liabilities	(8)	(11)
Change in assumptions underlying the present value of the scheme liabilities	715	(149)
Actuarial losses recognised in the STRGL	(44)	(21)

The cumulative actuarial loss recognised in the statement of total recognised gains and losses up to and including the financial year ended 30 June 2009 is €86,000 (2008: €42,000).

Where the charity is not a company and applies the SORP the amounts shown above would be included in the SOFA as Actuarial gains/losses on defined benefit schemes (D9).

The actual return on plan assets was:

	2009 €'000	2008 €'000
Actual return on plan assets	(253)	572

Expected contributions for the year ended 30 June 2010 are €300,000.

Movement in Scheme Assets and Liabilities	Scheme Assets €'000	Scheme Liabilities €'000	Pension* Deficit €'000
At 1 July 2007	6,252	(6,343)	(91)
Current Service Cost	-	(300)	(300)
Interest on scheme liabilities	-	(314)	(314)
Expected return on scheme assets	433	-	433
Actual less expected return on scheme assets	139	-	139
Experience losses on liabilities	-	(11)	(11)
Change in assumptions	-	(149)	(149)
Contributions by scheme participants	14	(14)	-
Benefits paid	(78)	78	-
Employer contributions paid	174	-	174
At 30 June 2008	6,934	(7,053)	(119)
Current Service Cost	-	(311)	(311)
Interest on scheme liabilities	-	(421)	(421)
Expected return on scheme assets	498	-	498
Actual less expected return on scheme assets	(751)	-	(751)
Experience losses on liabilities	-	(8)	(8)
Change in assumptions	-	715	715
Contributions by scheme participants	20	(20)	-
Benefits paid	(95)	95	-
Employer contributions paid	294	-	294
At 30 June 2009	6,900	(7,003)	(103)

All of the scheme liabilities above arise from schemes that are wholly or partly funded.

Risks and rewards arising from the assets

At 30 June 2009 the scheme assets were invested in a diversified portfolio that consisted primarily of equity and debt securities and properties. The fair value of the scheme assets as a percentage of total scheme assets and target allocations are set out below:

	Planned 2010*	2009	2008
(as a percentage of total scheme assets)	%	%	%
Equities	31	35	41
Bonds – Fixed interest fund	39	35	28
Property	30	30	31

Scheme assets do not include any property occupied by the charity.

Basis of expected rate of return on scheme assets

The fixed interest fund run by investment managers contains a mix of corporate bonds with different earnings potential. Thus a range of different assumptions have been used to estimate the expected return.

For equities the long-term rate of return is expected to exceed that of bonds by a margin, the "risk premium". In assessing the equity risk premium, past returns have been analysed giving a risk premium of 3% above the long-term gilt yields, giving an assumed return of 8%.

For property assets, the assumed rate of return is 7% reflecting an expectation that property returns will not match equity returns in the future. Thus, the overall expected return on scheme assets at 30 June 2009 is 6.9% (2007: 7.1%).

The principal actuarial assumptions at the balance sheet date:

	2009	2008
	%	%
Discount rate at 30 June	5.9	6.5
Future salary increases	2.5	5.0
Future pension increases	2.75	2.75
Inflation rate	1.6	2.6

Assumptions regarding future mortality are set based on advice from published statistics and experience.

The mortality assumptions are based on standard mortality tables which allow for future mortality improvements in the assumptions.

Longevity at 65 for current pensioners:

	2009	2008
Male	21.4	19.4
Female	23.1	22.4

Longevity at 65 for members retiring in 2034:

Male	XXX	XXX
Female	XXX	XXX

Note: All of the assumptions disclosed above are for illustrative purposes only and may not reflect current market place assumptions.

Amounts for the current and previous four years are as follows:

	2009	2008	2007	2006	2005
Present value of the scheme liabilities (€'000)	(7,176)	(7,131)	(6,343)	(6,181)	(6,001)
Fair value of scheme assets (€'000)	7,073	7,012	6,252	6,101*	5,934*
Pension deficit (€'000)	(103)	(119)	(91)	(80)	(67)
Experience adjustments on scheme liabilities as a percentage of scheme liabilities at the balance sheet date	0.1%	0.2%	2.3%	1.9%	1.2%
Experience adjustments on scheme assets as a percentage of scheme assets at the balance sheet date	(10.6)%	2.0%	1.3%	0.5%	0.5%

THE FUNDS OF THE CHARITY (E)

The structure of the funds of the charity and the accounting for   **5.76**
those funds is an important aspect of charity accounting. The
financial statements should provide a summary of the main
funds, differentiating between the unrestricted funds, restricted
and endowment funds. The types of funds of charities are shown
in **Figure 5.1** below:

Figure 5.1: The Types of Funds of Charities

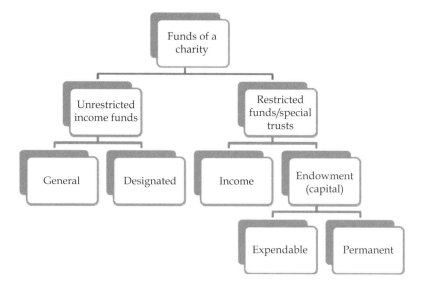

(SORP 2005, Figure 1, Page 11)

The notes to the financial statements should provide informa-   **5.77**
tion on the structure of the charity's funds. In particular, the
information provided should show:

(a) the assets representing each type of fund analysed between
    investments, fixed assets and current assets, unless the
    information is given in the balance sheet;
(b) disclosure of the purpose of the fund, how it arose and
    any restrictions imposed on the use of these funds;
(c) funds in deficit; and
(d) material transfers between funds and allocations to desig-
    nated funds should be separately disclosed, without net-
    ting off, and an explanation of the nature and reason for the
    transfer.

5.78　An example of the type of information to be disclosed in respect of funds is set out below.

Example – Statement of Funds

	Balance 1 July 2008 €000s	Total incoming resources €000s	Total resources expended €000s	Transfers €000s	Gains and Losses €000s	Balance 30 June 2009 €000s
Unrestricted funds:						
General reserve	1,500	30,000	(28,000)	150	-	3,650
Designated funds						
Tangible fixed asset fund:	500	-	-	(150)	-	350
Unrestricted funds	2,000	30,000	(28,000)	-	-	4,000
Restricted funds	5,000	12,000	(11,000)	-	-	6,000
Total funds	7,000	42,000	(39,000)	-	-	10,000

The transfer made between general and designated funds is made to match the net book value of fixed assets with a designated fund.

Restricted funds comprise the following unexpended balances on donations and grants given for specific purposes:

Charity restricted funds	Balance 1 July 2008 €000s	Total incoming resources €000s	Total resources expended €000s	Balance 30 June 2009 €000s
Irish Aid	2,700	2,583	(3,283)	2,000
European Community	2,000	3,975	(3,015)	2,960
Other Official Bodies	200	772	(762)	210
Other Donations and Appeals	100	4,670	(3,940)	830
Total		5,000	12,000	(11,000)	6,000

Analysis of assets and liabilities between funds

	Unrestricted funds		Restricted	Total
	General €000s	Designated €000s	Funds €000s	Funds €000s
Fund balances at 30 June 2009 are represented by:				
Tangible fixed assets	-	350	-	350
Current assets	5,288	-	6,000	11,288
Current liabilities	(1,638)	-	-	(1,638)
Fund balances at 30 June 2009	3,650	350	6,000	10,000
Fund balances at 30 June 2008	1,500	500	5,000	7,000

The designated fund comprises amounts set aside to finance the future depreciation on fixed assets. *Restricted funds* are those subject to specific restrictions imposed by donors or which have been raised by the charity for particular purposes, and the tables show those net assets at year end which can be attributed to restricted activities.

SHARE CAPITAL (E3a)

Some charities are incorporated with a share capital. Usually this is a nominal amount and the 'owner' of these shares is prohibited from benefiting from ownership of these shares. The share capital funds form part of restricted funds of the charity and, under company law, they must be shown separately on the balance sheet.   **5.79**

UNRESTRICTED INCOME FUNDS (E3b)

Unrestricted income funds are funds available to the charity trustees to apply for the general purposes of the charity. Income from assets held in an unrestricted fund will be unrestricted income.   **5.80**

REVALUATION RESERVE (E3c)

5.81   Charities that are companies are required to show the difference between the revalued amount of a fixed asset and its historic cost as a revaluation reserve in the balance sheet.

PENSION RESERVE (E3d)

5.82   The SORP requires charities to disclose a pensions reserve representing the asset or deficit on the defined benefit pension scheme.

Chapter 6

GRANT MAKING

INTRODUCTION

When grant making is a material part of a charity's activities, an **6.1**
accounting policy and an analysis of grants made is required to
be included in the financial statements.

Whether or not grant making is material to a charity's activities depends on the size of the charity and the importance of
grant-making activities to its overall activities. In accruals
accounting, only material items need to be reported. Earlier
SORPs, i.e. before SORP 2005, gave indicative materiality levels
for a number of disclosures, such as when grants to institutions should be disclosed. This approach has been replaced in
SORP 2005 with materiality being judged instead in the context of a particular disclosure rather than by using an arbitrary
threshold.

The SORP defines a *grant* as: **6.2**

> "any voluntary payment (or other transfer of property)
> in favour of a person or institution. Grant payments,
> when made by a charity, are any such voluntary payments
> made in furtherance of its objects. The payment or
> transfer may be for the general purposes of the recipient,
> or for some specific purpose such as the supply of a
> particular service. It may be unconditional, or be subject
> to conditions which, if not satisfied by the recipient, may
> lead to the grant, or property acquired with the aid of the
> grant, or part of it, being reclaimed."
>
> (SORP 2005, Appendix 1, GL 29)

COSTS ASSOCIATED WITH GRANT MAKING

6.3 Costs associated with the grant-making activity include the grants actually made and the support costs associated with the activity. Support costs to be included with grant making will include:

- costs incurred before grants are made, e.g. due diligence or research costs;
- costs incurred in monitoring grants to ensure they are used for the purposes of the grant agreement;
- costs or central overheads allocated on a fair and reasonable basis.

TYPES OF GRANT-MAKING ACTIVITIES

6.4 Grant-making charities may undertake their entire programme of charitable activities through grant-making activities. Other charities may undertake their activities through a combination of direct service provision and grant funding of third parties.

6.5 Grants made to individuals are for the direct benefit of the individual who receives the grant, for example an educational bursary to relieve financial hardship. Institutional grants are made directly to institutions, e.g. universities, hospitals, etc., or to individuals connected to these institutions. For example, a research grant to an individual connected to a university could be regarded as a grant to the university.

DISCLOSURE

6.6 The further information provided in the notes to the financial statements should provide the reader with an understanding of the nature of the activities or projects that are being funded. The information given should be such as to enable the user of the financial statements to understand how the grants made relate to the objects of the charity and the policy adopted by the trustees/directors in furtherance of those objects and whether the funding is provided directly to individuals or to assist an institution undertake its activities or projects.

6.7 The amounts of support costs associated with grant-making activities should be disclosed.

The SORP provides at paragraph 203 that: 6.8

"The analysis and explanation in the notes [to the financial state-
ments] should provide details, with amounts that reconcile with
the total of grants payable of:

(a) the total amount of grants analysed between grants to
    individuals and grants to institutions,
(b) an analysis of the total amount of grants paid by nature
    or type of activity or project being supported".

The information could be presented as set out at Table 6 of the   6.9
SORP:

SORP 2005 – Table 6. Analysis of grants

Analysis	Grants to Institutions Total amount €	Grants to Individuals Total amount €
Activity or Project 1 Activity or Project 2 Activity or Project 3		
Total		

In the case of institutional grants, information as to the   6.10
recipient(s) of the funding should be provided so that the reader
can appreciate the type and range of institutions supported.
The information being disclosed should give the name of the
institution and the total value of the grants made to that institution in the financial year under review. Where grants have been
made to an institution to fund different activities or purposes,
the total value of the grants for each activity or purpose should
be disclosed.

Information provided in relation to grant making may be lim-   6.11
ited or excluded when:

• grants are made to individuals – in which case details of the
  recipient are not required;

- grant-making activities in total are not material in the context of a charity's overall charitable activities – in which case no disclosures are required;
- total grants to a particular institution are not material in the context of institutional grants – in which case the name of the recipient institution need not be disclosed;
- disclosure of a particular institutional grant would seriously prejudice either the grant maker or recipient.

6.12   Where a charity withholds information where the circumstances amount to serious prejudice, the notes to the financial statements should disclose the total number and amount of grants made, the details of which have not been disclosed. The SORP also provides that full details of the grants not so disclosed should be provided to the charity's regulatory body together with an explanation of the reasons why such grants have not been disclosed. A statement that this disclosure has been made to the regulator is also required to be disclosed in the financial statements. In Ireland, a charity regulator has not yet been appointed.

GRANTS PAYABLE AND CONSTRUCTIVE OBLIGATIONS

6.13   Where a charity has a legal or constructive obligation in respect of a grant, a liability should be recognised in the charity's accounts. A constructive obligation arises under FRS 12 – Provisions and Contingent Liabilities and Contingent Assets – where events have created a valid expectation in other parties that the charity will discharge its obligations. A constructive obligation is likely to arise where:

(a) a specific commitment, or promise to provide goods, services, grant funding is given; and
(b) this is communicated directly to a beneficiary or grant recipient.

In such circumstances, the charity is unlikely to have a realistic alternative but to meet the obligation. The recognition of any resulting liability will be dependent on any conditions attaching to such commitments.

At paragraphs 154 to 160, the SORP sets out the requirements in respect of grants payable and constructive obligations. In the case of expenditure for and grants to beneficiaries in furtherance of a charity's charitable objects an exchange for consideration does not arise. A contractual or quasi-contractual relationship with the recipient of the grant or the charity's beneficiaries is not created. However, a liability may be created, which would need to be recognised. **6.14**

Each grant agreement and commitment will have to be reviewed to assess whether a liability and expenditure should be recorded. In situations where there are specific conditions to meet before a grant will be paid, then a liability would not be recognised until those conditions are met. The grant agreement should clearly state that further instalments will not be paid if certain conditions are not met. **6.15**

If the conditions to be met are outside of the grant-making charity's control, then a liability and expenditure should be recognised when the grant is committed.

If the conditions to be met remain within the control of the giving charity, the charity retains the discretion to avoid the expenditure and no liability would be recognised.

Each grant agreement, and the circumstances surrounding it, will need to be reviewed to determine the appropriate accounting treatment.

Paragraph 159 of the SORP sets out an example where a charity makes a specific commitment to grant fund a project over a three-year period and considers examples of situations that might arise as follows: **6.16**

"(a) If the multi-year grant obligation:
    (i) is conditional on an annual review of progress that determines whether future funding is provided; and
    (ii) discretion is retained by the giving charity to terminate the grant;
       then provided that evidence exists (e.g. from past review practice) that the discretion retained by the

charity has substance, this amounts to a condition and an immediate liability arises only for the first year of the funding commitment.

If the annual review process, although set out in the conditions of the grant, is not in practice used to determine whether funding is provided in the subsequent years of the commitment, then the review stipulation should not be interpreted as a condition and a liability for the full three years of the grant should be recognised.

(b) If there is no condition attaching to the grant that enables the charity to realistically avoid the commitment, the liability for the full three years of the funding should be recognised."

6.17 Where commitments contain conditions that are outside the charity's control, e.g. a donor may promise a grant payment on condition that the charity finds matching funding, a liability arises and expenditure should be recognised.

6.18 Where a liability has not been created because conditions have not been met, such a commitment should be disclosed as a contingent liability where the amounts are material.

Chapter 7

ALLOCATION OF COSTS

INTRODUCTION

The SORP provides that costs should be allocated to activities. **7.1**
Direct costs are usually easy to identify and should be allocated
to the activity giving rise to those costs. Indirect costs, on the
other hand, can be more difficult to analyse by activity. The
accounting systems and the way in which data is captured will
need to be planned so that detailed information on costs is readily available.

Costs should be captured in the accounting records by activity **7.2**
wherever possible. Where costs are incurred or shared over more
than one activity, a method of apportioning these costs over
those activities will need to be determined. The apportionment
of costs over activities should be consistent from one period to
the next and allocated on a reliable basis.

Charities need to balance the benefit to be obtained by the users **7.3**
of the financial statements, the beneficiaries and the charity itself
with the costs of providing this detailed information. The level
of detail provided should be proportionate to the size of the
charity and the complexity of its activities. The bases of apportionment of costs adopted should be appropriate to the charity's
circumstances and should be applied consistently from one
period to the next.

The notes to the financial statements should provide details of **7.4**
support costs and the way that these have been allocated to the
activities being undertaken by the charity. The SORP suggests a
layout for this disclosure at Table 4, which is reproduced below.

PRINCIPLES AND BASES OF COST ALLOCATION

The SORP at paragraphs 168 to 174 sets out the principles and **7.5**
bases for allocation of costs. Charities should ensure that the

SORP 2005 – Table 4. Example of Support Cost Breakdown by Activity

Support Cost (Examples)	Fundraising €	Activity 1 €	Activity 2 €	Activity 3 €	Activity 4 €	Activity 5 €	Basis of allocation
Management							Text describing method
Finance							Text describing method
Information Technology							Text describing method
Total							

bases for apportionment adopted are appropriate to the cost being apportioned and to the charity's circumstances.

In apportioning costs, the following principles should be applied:

- where appropriate the costs should be allocated directly to the activity giving rise to the cost;
- costs that are incurred over more than one activity should be apportioned over those activities on a reasonable, justifiable and consistent basis;
- depreciation, amortisation and impairment should be attributed in accordance with the same principles;
- support costs may not be attributable to a single activity but contribute to the overall organisational infrastructure that enables the activity to take place. These costs should be apportioned on a reasonable, justifiable and consistent basis to the activity cost categories being supported.

There are a number of bases for apportionment that may be   **7.6** applied. These include:

- usage
- per capita – number employed
- floor space occupied
- on the basis of time

DISCLOSURE

The accounting policies of the charity should explain the policy   **7.7** adopted for the apportionment of costs between activities and any estimation techniques used to calculate the apportionment (see below, **Chapter 9, paragraph 9.9,** item (c)).

A distinction should be made between publicity and information   **7.8** costs involved in raising the profile of the charity, which is associated with fundraising costs (costs of generating funds), and publicity and information that is provided in an educational manner in furtherance of the charity's objectives. Where a charity has any multipurpose activities and part of the costs are allocated to charitable activities, the policy for the identification of such multipurpose costs should be explained and the basis on which any allocation to charitable activities is made should be outlined.

Chapter 8

OTHER MATTERS TO BE COVERED IN THE NOTES TO THE FINANCIAL STATEMENTS

INTRODUCTION

This chapter deals with "other matters to be covered in the notes to the financial statements". The following matters are considered: **8.1**

- Related Party Transactions
- Trustee Remuneration and Benefits
- Trustees' Expenses
- Staff Costs and Emoluments
- Cost of Audit, Independent Examination or Reporting Accounting Services and other Financial Services
- Ex-gratia Payments
- Analysis of Net Movement in Funds.

RELATED PARTY TRANSACTIONS

The paragraphs in the SORP (paragraphs 221 to 229) reflect **8.2** the provisions of FRS 8 – Related Party Disclosures. Related party transactions take a variety of forms. Many of these transactions are entered into in the normal course of the charity's business. Others may be significant one-off transactions that may be at fair value on an arm's length basis, or which may be at some other amount that differs from market prices. The objective of the accounting standard, FRS 8, is to ensure that financial statements contain disclosures necessary to draw attention to the possibility that the reported financial position and results may have been affected by the existence of related parties and by material transactions with them (FRS 8, paragraph 1).

8.3   The SORP provides that:

> "disclosure in a note to the accounts is required of any transactions which the reporting charity or any institution connected with it ... has entered into with a related party. Such transactions might inhibit the charity from pursuing its own separate interests".

> (SORP 2005, paragraph 221)

Each charity must ensure that any decisions to enter into transactions are influenced only by the consideration of the charity's own interests.

Related Parties of Charities

8.4   *Related parties of charities* are defined in the Glossary to the SORP (GL 50) and include:

(a) any charity trustee and custodian trustee;

(b) any person or body who can appoint/remove trustees, direct trustees or whose consent the trustees require to exercise their discretion;

(c) any institution connected with the charity and any director of such institution;

(d) any other charity with which it is commonly controlled;

(e) any pension fund for the benefit of:
  (i) the employees of the charity, and/or
  (ii) of any other person who is a related party of the charity;

(f) any officer, agent or employee of the charity having authority or responsibility for directing or controlling the major activities or resources of the charity;

(g) any person connected to a person who is related to the charity.

Related Party Transactions

8.5   Related party transactions potentially include:

(a) purchases, sales, leases and donations (including donations which are made in furtherance of the charity's objects) of goods, property, money and other assets such as intellectual property rights to or from the related party;

(b) the supply of services by the related party to the charity and the supply of services by the charity to the related party;

(c) any other payments or other benefits which are made to trustees under express provisions of the governing document of a charity or in fulfilment of its charitable objectives.

FRS 8 requires disclosure of all transactions with related parties **8.6** that are material. Because, potentially, all related party transactions should be disclosed, the interpretation of what is material in this context is particularly important.

The FRS defines 'material' as follows: **8.7**

"Transactions are material when their disclosure might reasonably be expected to influence decisions made by the users of general purpose financial statements."

(FRS 8, paragraph 20)

FRS 8 also provides that: **8.8**

"The materiality of related party transactions is to be judged, not only in terms of their significance to the reporting entity, but also to their significance to the other related party when that party is:"

(a) a director, key manager or other individual in a position to influence, or accountable for stewardship of, the reporting entity; or

(b) a member of the close family of any individual mentioned in (a) above; or

(c) an entity controlled by any individual.

The SORP sets out the disclosures required in respect of related **8.9** party transactions. Material transactions should be disclosed regardless of whether or not they are undertaken on an arm's length basis. Any transaction with a trustee of the charity, or people connected with it, is always regarded as material, including trustee remuneration and other benefits. However, there may be circumstances where a transaction with a trustee need not be disclosed and these are discussed at **paragraph 8.12** below.

Disclosures

8.10   The following disclosures should be given in respect of related party transactions:

- the name(s) of the transacting related party or parties;
- a description of the relationship between the parties (including the interest of the related parties in the transaction);
- a description of the transaction;
- the amounts involved;
- outstanding balances with related parties at the balance sheet date and any provisions for doubtful debts from such persons;
- any amounts written off from such balances during the accounting year;
- any other elements of the transactions which are necessary for the understanding of the financial statements.

8.11   Disclosure can be given in aggregate for similar transactions and type of related party, unless individual disclosure is necessary to understand the impact on the financial statements or is a legal requirement.

Disclosures not required

8.12   The following related party transactions need not be disclosed, unless they are likely to influence the pursuance of the charity's separate independent interests:

- Donations received by the reporting charity from a related party, as long as the donor has not attached conditions that would or might require the charity to alter significantly the nature of its existing activities if it were to accept the donation. (**Note**, however, that any material grant by the reporting charity to a charity which is a related party should be disclosed.)
- Minor or routine unremunerated services provided to the charity.

- Contracts of employment between the charity and its employees (unless the employees are the charity trustees or people connected with them).
- The purchase from the charity by a related party of minor articles that are offered for sale to the public on the same terms.
- The provision of services to a related party (including a charity trustee or person connected with a charity trustee) where the related party receives the services as part of a wider beneficiary class and on the same terms as other members of the class.
- The payment or reimbursement of out-of-pocket expenses to a related party (including a charity trustee or a person connected with a charity trustee).

TRUSTEE REMUNERATION AND BENEFITS

Trustees and directors of charities do not generally receive remu- **8.13** neration or other benefits from the charities for which they are responsible, or from institutions connected with those charities. Accordingly, where any transactions are entered into with charity trustees or persons connected to a charity trustee, detailed disclosures of the remuneration and benefits should be disclosed.

Where transactions take place with trustees or persons connected with charity trustees they should always be considered material unless one of the exemptions at **paragraph 8.12** above applies.

The SORP provides that each type of related party transaction should be disclosed. In the case of remuneration this means that the amount paid to each trustee should be disclosed separately. This disclosure should also be given in respect of any pension arrangements made for individual trustees.

Where no remuneration or other benefits are paid to trustees, or persons connected with them, this fact should be stated.

TRUSTEE EXPENSES

8.14   Where the charity has met the expenses incurred by trustees for services provided to the charity, either by way of reimbursement or by way of allowance to the trustee or by way of payment to a third party, the aggregate amount of these expenses should be disclosed in the financial statements. Details of the nature of the expenses and the number of trustees involved should be disclosed. Where trustees act as agent on behalf of the charity and are reimbursed for that expenditure there is no need to disclose that expenditure. Routine expenditure that is attributable collectively to the services provided by trustees, e.g. room hire, also does not need to be disclosed.

8.15   Where no expenses are paid to trustees, this fact should be disclosed.

STAFF COSTS AND EMOLUMENTS

8.16   The notes to the financial statements should disclose details of staff costs. The SORP provides that these should be disclosed whether or not the charity itself incurs these costs. Where a connected or independent company/organisation employs and remunerates the employees who work in the charity the nature of the arrangement and the amounts involved should be disclosed. This applies also where arrangements are in place with third parties for the provision of staff.

8.17   The total of staff costs should be disclosed, analysing it between gross wages and salaries, employers' national insurance costs and pension contributions for the year. The average number of staff employed should be disclosed and where there are significant numbers of part-time staff the average number of whole-time equivalents should be disclosed. This information should be analysed over sub-headings appropriate to the charity's activities. Where a charity is a company, the disclosures required under company law should be included in the notes to the financial statements.

COST OF AUDIT, INDEPENDENT EXAMINATION OR REPORTING ACCOUNTANT SERVICES AND OTHER FINANCIAL SERVICES

The SORP requires that the notes to the financial statements **8.18** should disclose separately the amounts paid to the auditor, independent examiner or reporting accountant in respect of:

(a) the costs of their external scrutiny; and

(b) other financial services such as taxation advice, consultancy, financial advice and accountancy.

EX-GRATIA PAYMENTS

Ex-gratia payments are payments that the trustees of a charity **8.19** believe that they have a compelling moral obligation to make and are not made as an application of funds or property of the charity. These payments should be disclosed in the notes to the financial statements. Where the authority of the courts, the Attorney General or Charity Regulator is obtained to make such payments, this fact should be disclosed.

ANALYSIS OF THE NET MOVEMENT IN FUNDS

The net movement in funds of a charity represents the increase **8.20** or decrease in funds of the charity and may not necessarily be an indicator of performance of the charity.

Charities may invest in fixed assets from which to provide services or make investments of a programme or social related nature. Charities may also receive gifts of an endowed nature, which are not available to finance expenditure.

Information on the funds of the charity and the movement on these funds can be valuable information for the user of the charity's financial statements in helping them understand the resources available to the charity and should be disclosed.

The SORP suggests that a charity may choose to disclose the fol- **8.21** lowing information in the notes to the financial statements:

"(a) total net movement in funds for the year;

(b) net endowment receipts for the year (value of endowment receipts less any release of expendable endowment to income funds);

(c) net expenditure on additions to functional fixed assets (cost of additions less proceeds of any disposals) for the year; and

(d) net investment in programme related investments (cost of additions less proceeds of any disposals) for the year."

(SORP 2005, paragraph 243)

Chapter 9

ACCOUNTING POLICIES

INTRODUCTION

Charities are required to select accounting policies that are **9.1** appropriate to their circumstances. Accounting policies are appropriate if they are:

- **Relevant** – providing information on a timely basis that has an ability to influence economic decisions of users of information.
- **Reliable** – presenting information that fairly reflects the transactions, ensuring it is free from material bias and, where conditions are uncertain, has been prudently estimated.
- **Comparable** – information is useful if it can be compared with similar information on the charity at some other period and against other charities. Such comparability can generally be achieved through consistent application of accounting policies and disclosure of those policies.
- **Understandable** – for information to be useful, it must be presented in such a way that users with a reasonable knowledge of business and economic activities and accounting and also a willingness to study the information can understand and interpret that information.

Disclosure of Basis of Preparation

The notes to the financial statements should set out the basis of **9.2** preparation indicating whether they have been prepared in accordance with accounting standards generally accepted in Ireland, whether they comply with the UK Charities SORP, and the Companies Acts 1963 to 2009. (**Note**: the provisions of the Companies Act 1986 do not generally apply to charities, as charity companies do not trade for the acquisition of gain by the members.)

Disclosure of Accounting Policies

9.3   FRS 18 requires disclosure of the accounting polices, applied in the preparation of the financial statements, in the notes to the financial statements. A description of each of the accounting policies that is material in the context of the financial statements should be provided. The purpose of this disclosure is to enable users of the financial statements to understand the accounting policies applied in the preparation of the financial statements.

9.4   In certain circumstances, it may be necessary for a charity to depart from an accounting standard. If the accounts depart from an accounting standard in any material respect, this should be disclosed in the accounting policies and the reason for the departure should be explained together with the financial impact. A departure from an accounting standard should only be made where it is necessary to ensure that the financial statements give a true and fair view. Departures from accounting standards are not acceptable simply because of cost/benefit considerations.

Reviewing and Changing Accounting Policies

9.5   Accounting policies should be reviewed regularly to ensure that they remain the most appropriate (FRS 18, paragraph 45). An accounting policy should not be changed unless the new policy is more appropriate to the charity's circumstances. A material change arising from a change in accounting policy will give rise to a prior year adjustment unless another accounting standard, UITF or companies legislation, requires otherwise.

Estimation Techniques

9.6   Estimation techniques are required in certain situations to apply an accounting policy. They are used as a proxy for making best estimates where the value of the items being measured is unknown. Estimation techniques may be used in the following situations:

- for determining the useful life of fixed assets and appropriate depreciation rates;
- as methods and principles of allocating costs to activities;
- estimating provisions for bad debts where charities are in receipt of income for delivery of services or trading;

- for determining the cost of inventories in the case of charities that produce and trade in goods;
- determination of provisions against inventories;
- impairment of fixed assets and financial assets;
- valuation of fixed assets, particularly historic or heritage assets.

The selected estimation techniques should enable the financial statements to give a true and fair view and they should be consistent with the requirements of the accounting standards.

Specific Policies

The trustees should disclose in the notes to the financial state-   **9.7**
ments the accounting policies that they have adopted in respect
of material items included in the financial statements. The SORP
sets out examples of matters for which accounting policies
should be explained where the amounts included in the financial statements are material. Paragraphs 362 to 370 of the SORP
(reproduced below) set out examples of situations where further
information may be required.

Incoming resources policy notes

The accounting policy adopted for each material source of   **9.8**
income should be disclosed. The basis of recognition will normally be on a receivable basis but in some cases further
explanation may be required. The SORP sets out the following
examples:

"(a) a description of when a legacy is regarded as receivable;
(b) The basis of recognition of gifts in kind and donated services and facilities, specifically covering when such items
are not included in the Statement of Financial Activities
and the methods of valuation;
(c) the basis of recognition of grants receivable, including
those for fixed assets, and how the grants are analysed
between the different types of incoming resources;
(d) whether any incoming resources are deferred and the
basis for any deferrals;
(e) the basis for including subscriptions for life membership;

(f) whether the incoming resources from endowment funds are unrestricted or restricted;

(g) whether any incoming resources have been included in the Statement of Financial Activities net of expenditure and the reason for this."

(SORP 2005, paragraph 362)

Resources expended policy notes

9.9 The accounting policy notes in respect of resources expended should explain how material items of resources expended have been treated in the financial statements. These policy notes may include:

"(a) The policy for the recognition of liabilities including constructive obligations should be given. Where the liabilities are included as provisions, the point at which the provision is considered to become binding and the basis of any discount factors used in current value calculations for long term commitments should be given. This is particularly applicable to grants, the policy for which should be separately identified.

(b) The policy for including items within the relevant activity categories of resources expended should be given. In particular the policy for including items within:

    i. costs of generating funds;
    ii. charitable activities;
    iii. governance costs.

(c) The methods and principles for the allocation and apportionment of all costs between the different activity categories of resources expended in (b). This disclosure should include the underlying principle, i.e. whether based on staff time, staff salaries, and space occupied or other. Where the costs apportioned are material, then further clarification on the method of apportionment used is necessary, including the proportions used to undertake the calculations."

(SORP 2005, paragraph 363)

Asset policy notes

The policy for capitalisation of fixed assets for charity use should   **9.10**
be stated including:

(a) whether the asset is accounted for at cost, valuation or
    revalued amount and the method of valuation, if
    appropriate;
(b) whether heritage assets are capitalised and the basis of
    value if they are capitalised. If they are not capitalised,
    the reason for non-capitalisation should be disclosed;
(c) the basis of depreciation and the rates/useful lives of
    fixed assets;
(d) the policy in relation to impairment reviews.

(SORP 2005, paragraph 364)

The policy for including investments in the accounts should be   **9.11**
given. This should be at market value but may need to be modi-
fied for the valuation of:

(a) investments not listed on a recognised stock exchange;
(b) investment properties; and
(c) investments in subsidiary undertakings.

(SORP 2005, paragraph 365)

The basis of inclusion in the Statement of Financial Activities   **9.12**
(SOFA) of unrealised and realised gains and losses on investments should be stated.

The basis of inclusion of stocks and work in progress (where   **9.13**
relevant the amount of unsold or unused goods and materials
should be given).

Funds' structure policy notes

The different types of funds held by the charity should be   **9.14**
described, including the policy for any transfers between funds
and allocations to or from designated funds. The movement of
funds may include situations where there is a release of restricted
or endowed funds to unrestricted funds or charges are made

from the unrestricted to other funds. The policy for determining each designated fund should be stated.

Other policy notes

9.15 "These could include policies for the recognition of the following:

>   (a) pension costs and any pension asset or liability;
>   (b) foreign exchange gains and losses;
>   (c) treatment of exceptional items;
>   (d) treatment of finance and operating leases;
>   (e) treatment of irrecoverable VAT."

GOING CONCERN

9.16 The FRS 5 provides that an entity should prepare its financial statements on a going concern basis, *unless*:
- the entity is being liquidated or has ceased trading; or
- the directors intend to liquidate or cease trading or have no realistic alternative but to do so.

9.17 In preparing financial statements on a going concern basis assets and liabilities are recorded on the basis that their carrying value will be recovered or discharged in the normal course of the charity's business.

9.18 It is generally understood that in adopting the going concern concept that the trustees/directors of the charity are satisfied that the charity will continue in operational existence for the foreseeable future. The foreseeable future should cover a period of at least 12 months from date of approval of the financial statements by the trustees/directors.

9.19 Where the trustees/directors have identified material uncertainties related to events or conditions that may cast significant doubt about the ability of the charity to continue as a going concern and the trustees/directors consider the going concern basis remains appropriate, disclosures explaining the nature of the uncertainties and the reasons why they believe the going concern basis remains appropriate should be included in the notes to the financial statements.

Where the trustees/directors believe that the going concern basis **9.20**
is not appropriate or a decision has been made to cease activities
or liquidate the charity, disclosures explaining the basis of the
conclusion and the accounting policies adopted in preparing the
financial statements on a basis other than the going concern basis
should be included in the financial statements. Where there are
any uncertainties about the carrying value of assets and liabilities these should also be set out.

Chapter 10

CONSOLIDATION

CONSOLIDATION OF SUBSIDIARY UNDERTAKINGS

10.1 Where a charity has subsidiary undertakings, these should be consolidated in accordance with the provisions of FRS 2 – Accounting for Subsidiary Undertakings. The principles set out in FRS 2 should be followed by all charities regardless of whether or not they are companies. The definition of a parent and subsidiary undertaking is set out in the Glossary (Appendix 1) to SORP 2005 at GL 44 as:

> "In relation to a charity, an undertaking is the parent undertaking of another undertaking, called a subsidiary undertaking, where the charity controls the subsidiary. Control requires that the parent can both direct and derive benefit from the subsidiary.
>
> (a) Direction is achieved if the charity or its trustees:
>
> > (i) hold or control a majority of the voting rights, or
> > (ii) have the right to appoint or remove a majority of the board of directors or trustees of the subsidiary undertaking, or
> > (iii) have the power to exercise, or actually exercise, a dominant influence over the subsidiary undertaking, or
> > (iv) manage the charity and the subsidiary on a unified basis.
>
> (b) Benefits derived can either be economic benefits that result in a net cash inflow to the charity or can arise through the provision of goods or services to the benefit of the charity or its beneficiaries."

10.2 Paragraphs 381 to 406 of the SORP provide detailed guidance on how to account for subsidiary undertakings within the consolidated financial statements of a parent undertaking. Reference should be made to Irish company law where the charity is an incorporated entity.

CONSOLIDATION OF ASSOCIATES, JOINT VENTURES AND JOINT ARRANGEMENTS

10.3 Associates, joint ventures and joint arrangements should be accounted for under FRS 9 – Associates, Joint Ventures and Joint Undertakings. Where a charity has a long-term participating interest in another and exercises significant influence over its operating and financial policy, that interest is likely to be an associate undertaking.

10.4 In certain situations, charities that make grants to other entities may also provide financial advice or be appointed to boards of trustees/directors. In situations where this position gives the grant-making charity significant influence over the operational and financial policies of the recipient, that interest may be an associate undertaking.

10.5 Where control is equally shared between two entities, a joint venture arrangement may exist. This can arise even if one of the parties holds 20% or more of the beneficial voting rights but the management arrangements may be such that control is clearly shared between the entities. In those cases, a joint venture arrangement may exist.

10.6 Charities sometimes undertake activities in partnership with other entities without setting up a separate legal entity. These are referred to as *joint arrangements* and the notes to the financial statements should provide appropriate details of the arrangements and the charity's commitments under those arrangements.

Chapter 11

CASH FLOW STATEMENTS

INTRODUCTION

FRS 1 – Cash Flow Statements – applies for all charities except **11.1**
where they can avail of the exemptions set out in FRS 1. The
principal objective of FRS 1 is to require reporting entities falling
within its scope to:

- report their cash generation and cash absorption for a
  period by highlighting the significant components of cash
  flow in a way that facilitates comparison of the cash flow
  performances of different businesses;
- provide information that assists in the assessment of their
  liquidity, solvency and financial adaptability.

In the case of charities, these objectives are interpreted as a
requirement to show the cash received and used by the charity
in the accounting period.

EXEMPTIONS FROM PREPARING CASH FLOW STATEMENTS

FRS 1 requires all reporting entities that prepare financial state- **11.2**
ments intended to give a true and fair view of their financial
position and profit or loss (or income and expenditure) to include
a cash flow statement as a *primary* statement within their financial statements, unless specifically exempted. Companies
incorporated under the Companies Acts and entitled to the
exemptions for small companies when filing financial statements
with the Registrar of Companies are entitled to avail of the
exemption. The FRS also provides that entities that would have
met the 'small company' limits if they were companies can also
avail of this exemption.

As set out in **paragraph 11.2,** a company availing of the 'small' **11.3**
company status allowed under the Companies (Amendment)

Act 1986 will not have to prepare a cash flow statement in accordance with FRS 1. However, this exemption may not extend to a company limited by guarantee and therefore these companies would have to prepare a cash flow regardless of company size.

Many companies limited by guarantee fall outside of the scope of the Companies (Amendment) Act 1986, as these companies are commonly used for the incorporation of entities "not trading for the acquisition of gain by the members". Companies "not trading for the acquisition of gain by the members" are excluded from the provisions of that Act.

11.4   Most small reporting entities are exempt from the requirement to include a cash flow statement as part of their financial statements. The scope of this exemption is currently being re-examined as part of a wider examination of the reporting requirements for small entities. However, the ASB encourages small reporting entities to include a cash flow statement as part of their financial statements if it would provide useful information to users of those financial statements and the benefits of the exercise outweigh the costs.

FORMAT OF CASH FLOW STATEMENTS

11.5   Charities should follow the formats set out in FRS 1 and the analysis of the cash movements should accord with the charity's operations as reflected in the SOFA. An entity's cash flow statement should list its cash flows for the period classified under the following standard headings:

- Operating activities
- Dividends from joint ventures and associates
- Returns on investments and servicing of finance
- Taxation
- Capital expenditure and financial investment
- Acquisitions and disposals
- Equity dividends paid
- Management of liquid resources; and financing.

In situations where the presentation set out above would not   **11.6**
present fairly the activities of the charity, the cash flow statement should disclose separately, where material, the individual
cash flows under those headings and an alternative presentation
should be devised to show other cash flows. This situation is
expected to be rarely encountered in practice.

The SORP does not required or recommend a columnar   **11.7**
approach to the cash flow statement.

INDEX